Classic Cocktail Guides
and Retro Bartender Books

What to Drink

Non-Alcoholic Drinks and Cocktails
Served During Prohibition

Bertha E. L. Stockbridge

Historic Cookbooks of the World
Kalevala Books, Chicago

*"Temperance is moderation in the things that are good and total
abstinence from the things that are foul."*
— Frances E. Willard (1839–1898)

What to Drink
Non-Alcoholic Drinks and Cocktails
Served During Prohibition

Joanne Asala, Editor
Historic Cookbooks of the World

Rowan Grier, Series Editor
Classic Cocktail Guides
and Retro Bartender Books

Classic Cocktail Guides and Retro Bartender Books and *Historic
Cookbooks of the World* are published by Kalevala Books, an imprint of
Compass Rose Technologies, Inc., PO Box 409095, Chicago, IL 60640.
Titles published by Kalevala Books are available at special quantity
discounts to use as premiums and sales promotions or for academic
use. For more information, please write to the Director of Special Sales,
Compass Rose Technologies, Inc., PO Box 409095, Chicago, IL 60640 or
contact us through our Web site, www.CompassRose.com.

Editors' Note

Some ingredients found in vintage cookbooks are unavailable or hard
to come by today. Check out our resource guide at the back for vendors
who specialize in hard-to-find ingredients.

ISBN: 978-1-880954-36-2

WHAT TO DRINK

THE BLUE BOOK OF BEVERAGES

RECIPES AND DIRECTIONS FOR MAKING AND SERVING
NON-ALCOHOLIC DRINKS FOR ALL OCCASIONS

BY

BERTHA E. L. STOCKBRIDGE

AUTHOR OF THE LIBERTY COOK BOOK

D. APPLETON AND COMPANY
NEW YORK   LONDON

1920

PRINTED IN THE UNITED STATES OF AMERICA

TO

MY LITTLE DAUGHTER,

JANET J. O. STOCKBRIDGE,

THIS BOOK IS DEDICATED,
WITH MY DEEPEST LOVE

OMAR UP TO DATE

A box of chocolates underneath a bough,
An ice cream cone, some lemonade, and thou
Beside me singing in the wilderness
Make prohibition Paradise enow.

ANONYMOUS

FOREWORD

The hostess of to-day will be called upon to serve drinks in her home more than formerly, I imagine, and it were well to go back to the habits and customs of our grandmothers and be prepared to serve a refreshing drink in an attractive manner at a moment's notice.

To do this, one needs have a stock of syrups, either homemade or commercial, as well as a supply of shrubs and vinegars on hand.

To-day's hostess does not hold up her hands in horror crying that she knows nothing of preparing these things, for she has learned a great deal about canning and preserving in the last few years, so making syrups, vinegars and shrubs will seem like child's play. If, however, she is inclined to think it an arduous task, let her turn to these recipes, and she will be convinced that the labor and the time expended bring their own reward in the satisfaction gained by knowing that one has served a delicious drink delightfully made.

There may be the feeling, if my hostess lives in an apartment, that there is not room enough to store these syrups and vinegars, and while that may be true in part, it is always possible to keep two or three popular syrups in quart bottles, and at least one bottle of fruit vinegar, in the refrigerator.

As both syrups and vinegars may be made in small quantities, one may make them oftener and make enough to last a week or two.

There are one or two things I would impress upon the hostess who would be popular, and if I refer to these things again in the book, I trust I may be pardoned, for they are most imperative.

First: the necessity for selecting attractive glassware, which need not be expensive, but should be thin and clear, and, when in use, should always be polished.

When purchasing linen, select it because of its daintiness rather than for its elaborateness. Plate doylies and serviettes which are plain and fine may be purchased for a very little money if care is taken. Who would not rather use a doylie with a button-holed edge, spotlessly clean, than one heavily embroidered which will require three times the labor to launder?

If drinks are served by the maid, it is as essential that her cuffs, collar, cap and apron be as spotless as the doylies on the service plates.

When cold drinks are served, be sure that the glasses are chilled.

For hot drinks, heat the cups or glasses before pouring the drinks.

Place the glass or cup on a doylie on a small plate.

When serving an invalid, be over-particular; the glass must shine, the doylie be spotless, and the plate the most attractive obtainable. If it is possible lay a flower on the plate or tray before it is sent into the ill one's room.

The appetite of a very finicky person may be tempted by this over-carefulness.

BERTHA E. L. STOCKBRIDGE.

NEW YORK

CONTENTS

MEASURES

I wish to emphasize the absolute necessity for accurate measuring; to be a successful mixer of drinks, one must measure as carefully as one should when cooking. I use the measures I have in my kitchen, and have used them in making these recipes. Surely one has a quart cup, a half

MEASURING SPOONS

pint, or one cup, measure and a set of spoons; the tablespoon, dessertspoon, teaspoon and half teaspoon. Some sets have the quarter-teaspoon too. These sets, made of aluminum, may be purchased in any hardware store, or in the housekeeping department in the large shops at very reasonable prices. The glass cup is marked for quarter, half

GLASS MEASURING CUPS

and three-quarters on one side, while on the reverse the marking is for one-third and two-thirds. The quart cup is marked for quarter, half and three-quarters; each quarter being equal to one cupful.

The housekeeper who becomes accustomed to using *exact* measurements will never return to the hit-or-miss plan, because she will be sure that every time she mixes a drink

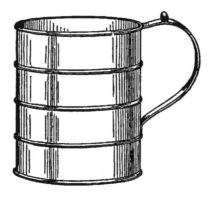

QUART MEASURE

or makes a syrup or a cream that it will be just as she wishes it to be.

HOUSEHOLD SCALES

WHAT TO DRINK

I—FRUITADES, ICED, FRAPPÉ AND HOT

There are a number of things worth considering when serving drinks at home; first among these is the use of attractive glassware. Good looking glasses cost no more than ugly ones, and clear fine glass polishes better than heavy blurred glass. And surely any drink is more pleasing to the palate if the eye is pleased. Be sure that the glasses shine, and also ascertain that glasses meant to hold cold drinks are chilled. Almost all fruitades, no matter what the name or foundation, contain lemon juice, so it is also well to remember that lemons intended for squeezing should be peeled, and that very carefully. While the lemon peel, or the zest, rather, is an excellent flavor, it is not satisfactory in lemonade, as there is a little bitterness when it stands, which displeases some people.

Most of the recipes given for these fruitades are for individual drinks, to make it easier for the hostess to ascertain how much to prepare if she knows the number of people to be served.

A cocktail shaker, an ice shaver and a long-handled spoon are almost a necessity in making drinks. They are at least a great aid, and as none of these things is expensive and all may be obtained in the housekeeping department of any city shop, or in the hardware store in small towns, there seems no reason for not owning them.

Fruitades are delicious, refreshing and healthful, and surely not difficult to make, so that the gracious hostess will serve these cooling drinks often.

1

If syrups are made and bottled one need not worry about serving a delectable drink in a surprisingly short time.

BASEBALL LEMONADE

For an individual drink, use:

1 egg,
1 lemon,
1 spoonful of sugar,
⅔ cupful of milk,
½ cupful of water.

Put the egg in the bottom of the tall glass; add the juice of a lemon, a spoonful of sugar, a little ice, shaved fine, and the milk and water. Put into a shaker, shake well and serve.

EGG LEMONADE

⅔ cupful of finely shaved ice,
1 egg,
3 teaspoonfuls of powdered sugar,
⅔ cupful of water,
   Juice of one lemon,
   Carbonated water.

Use either a large glass and a shaker top, or a cocktail shaker. Place all the ingredients in the shaker except the carbonated water, shake well, pour into an attractive glass, add the carbonated water, and serve.

FRUIT LEMONADE

1 lemon,
1 slice of orange,
1 cherry,
1 slice of pineapple,
1 Malaga grape,
2 teaspoonfuls of sugar,
   Shaved ice,
   Water.

Put the juice of the lemon, sugar, shaved or cracked ice, and water enough to make a glass full in a shaker, shake well, pour into a tall glass, and add the fruit and serve at once.

GRAPE JUICE LEMONADE

3 lemons,
1 pint of grape juice,
1½ pints of water,
1 cupful of sugar.

Place a small square of ice in a tall glass pitcher; mix the lemon juice, sugar, water and grape juice together, pour into the pitcher; allow to become thoroughly chilled and serve.

GINGER ALE LEMONADE

3 lemons,
1 pint of ginger ale,
1½ pints of water,
1 cupful of sugar.

Place a goodly sized piece of ice in a glass pitcher and pour over it the juice of the lemons, sugar and water, which should have been thoroughly mixed. Stir and when the sugar is dissolved, add the ginger ale. This should be served without delay, while the " fizz " is still in the ginger ale.

It is not at all necessary to use imported ginger ales, as there are domestic makes which are equally as good.

GRAPEFRUIT AND ORANGEADE

1 grapefruit,
2 oranges,
1 cupful of sugar,
1 pint of ginger ale,
1 pint of water,
1 pint of crushed ice,
1 full spray of mint.

Cut the grapefruit in half and extract the juice by using a large glass orange juice extractor. Extract the orange juice, add sugar and allow to stand for an hour if possible, stirring occasionally. When ready to serve, add crushed ice, water and ginger ale, stir and add the spray of mint well crushed. Serve while it still has a sparkle.

MINT GINGER ALE

1 pint of ginger ale,
1 lemon,
2 sprays of mint.

For this refreshing drink, crush the mint and put into a tall glass pitcher, add the crushed ice, the juice of half a lemon and the thinly sliced second half. Add the ginger ale, stir with a long handled spoon and serve at once.

ORANGE GRAPEADE

1 orange,
½ pint of chipped or shaved ice,
½ pint of grape juice,
   Sugar.

Extract the juice from the orange and add to the grape juice, stir and add the shaved ice. If not sweet enough add sugar to taste.

LIMEADE

2 fresh limes,
1½ teaspoonfuls of sugar,
   Spring or carbonated water,
   Mint,
   Ice.

Extract the juice from the limes, put into a tall straight-sided glass and add sugar or plain syrup. If sugar is used, stir until the sugar is dissolved. Add water to fill the glass and stir, or carbonated water, and put a spray of mint into each service. Serve with a straw.

LIMEADE WITH LIME SYRUP

½ lemon,
2 tablespoonfuls of lime syrup,
2 tablespoonfuls of plain syrup,
  Carbonated water or spring water,
  Ice.

Extract the juice from the half lemon, put into a tall glass,
add lime syrup and plain syrup and stir, then add the carbonated water, or spring water, if desired.   Mint or a cherry
may be added as liked.

TEA-RHUBARBADE

6 stalks of young rhubarb,
1 lemon,
2 oranges,
1 quart of water,
1 pint of tea,
  Sugar.

Wash the rhubarb and cut into inch lengths, add a quart
of water and stew until tender; drain, and set the juice away
to cool.   (The pulp may be used for tarts or marmalade.)
Add a pint of tea to the strained rhubarb; extract the lemon
juice and add this and the oranges thinly sliced.   Sweeten
to taste and pour over shaved ice in tall thin glasses.

CRÉOLE "FROG" LEMONADE

2 dozen lemons,
1 pound of sugar,
2 quarts of water,
2 quarts of Seltzer,
1 pineapple,
3 dozen strawberries.

Use a large punch bowl; put the sugar, lemon juice and
water in it, and stir well until the sugar is dissolved; add
the juice of one pineapple and the Seltzer water.   Mix well
again and add the strawberries, slices of pineapple and

very thin slices of lemon. Place a large piece of ice in the center of the bowl, and allow to stand until very cold before serving.

CANTON LEMONADE

½ cupful of lemon juice,
1¼ cupfuls of sugar,
1 pint of water,
½ teaspoonful of ground ginger.

Mix the sugar, ginger and water and boil until slightly syrup-like, then add the lemon juice. Cool and dilute as desired, or bottle hot for use when needed. Use two tablespoonfuls to a small glass of iced water when ready to serve.

ORANGE-LEMONADE

1 lemon,
1 quart of water,
3 oranges,
1 cupful of white grape juice,
   Sugar.

Wash the oranges, and rub a cube of sugar over the skin of one orange; cut the oranges and extract the juice, adding just enough sugar to make slightly sweet. To this add the juice of one lemon, stir, add the water, then the grape juice and serve at once.

PLAIN LEMONADE

½ cupful of lemon juice,
1¼ cupfuls of sugar,
1 pint of water.

Boil the water and sugar together until syrup-like; take from the fire and add the lemon juice. Cool and dilute as desired, the strength depending upon the taste of those to be served. To dilute one may use cracked ice, iced water, or Apollinaris, or a mixture of water and Apollinaris.

APOLLINARIS LEMONADE

2 tablespoonfuls of lemon juice,
¼ teaspoonful of sugar,
  Apollinaris,
  Cracked ice.

Put the lemon juice, sugar, cracked ice and Apollinaris in a shaker, shake for a minute, pour into a tall, thin glass and serve at once.

WHITE GRAPE JUICE LEMONADE

1 pint of water,
1 lemon,
1 cupful of white grape juice,
  Sugar,
  Shaved ice.

Usually the white grape juice is sweet enough to serve with the lemon juice without using sugar, depending always upon the person to be served. Cut a lemon in two, extract the juice from half, and slice the other half very thin. Mix the lemon juice with the sugar, if any is to be used, first trying a teaspoonful, add the water, stir until the sugar is dissolved, add the grape juice and then the thinly sliced half lemon, stir and serve.

ORGEAT LEMONADE

1 tablespoonful of powdered sugar,
1 tablespoonful of orgeat syrup (see syrups)
¼ lemon,
  Ice,
  Berries.

Fill the shaker about one-third full of shaved ice, pour over it the syrup and the lemon juice; fill to three quarters full with water; shake, add any berries in season; pour into a thin tall glass and serve at once.

RASPBERRY LEMONADE

    1 quart of water,
    1 lemon,
    1 pint of raspberries,
    ½ cupful of sugar,
      Ice.

Select a half-cupful of nice firm berries, and put aside, then crush the remaining berries, and press through a fine cloth. Extract the juice from the lemon, add to the berry juice, add shaved ice, sugar and water and shake well. Pour into a glass pitcher and add the selected whole berries and serve.

ITALIAN LEMONADE

    ½ lemon,
    ½ orange,
    1 teaspoonful of powdered sugar,
    1 cupful of ice,
    1 tablespoonful of white grape juice,
      Fruits in season,
    1 spoonful of ice cream.

Put the juice of half a lemon and half an orange into a shaker with the sugar and cracked ice and shake until the ice is well melted. Pour into a tall thin glass, fill with iced water, stir, add small fruits in season, and top with a teaspoonful of ice cream.

SODA LEMONADE

    ½ lemon,
    1 teaspoonful of sugar,

½ cupful of cracked ice,
Plain soda.

Put the juice of half a lemon and the sugar into a tall glass with the ice, stir with a long handled spoon, using the left hand; pour in the soda with the right.   Serve at once.

STRAWBERRY LEMONADE

½ lemon,
1 teaspoonful of sugar,
1 dozen large strawberries,
½ cupful of shaved ice,
   Milk.

Fill a shaker about a third full of ice; (about a half cupful) add the juice of a half lemon, the juice from a dozen strawberries, and the sugar.   Shake well, add enough milk to nearly fill the shaker, and strain into a tall glass.

FRUITADES AND SODAS FROM JUICES OF CANNED FRUITS

So often when a can of strawberries is opened, we find there is an abundance of juice, more in fact than we care to use with the berries on the table, and if the desired amount, *only,* is left with the fruit for table consumption, and the rest reserved, many combinations which are tasty and desirable may be made without the extra expense of purchasing fruits or prepared syrups.

Strawberries are not the only berries from which the juice may be taken, for blackberries and raspberries, both red and black, are equally desirable.   Besides these berries, there is no good reason why the juice from plums, pineapples, cherries and peaches may not be used to as good advantage.

STRAWBERRY SODA

Carbonated water,
Cream,
Strawberry juice or syrup.

We are more likely to have iced tea glasses in our homes than the regulation soda glasses, and for that reason I advise using them in preparing a home-made soda.

Pour enough strawberry juice into a glass to fill it one-third full, add three tablespoonfuls of thick cream, and fill with carbonated water.

BLACKBERRYADE

¼ glass of blackberry juice,
1 teaspoonful of lemon juice,
1 teaspoonful of powdered sugar,
　Cracked ice,
　Water.

Put the one-fourth glassful (iced tea glass) of blackberry juice, the lemon juice, sugar and cracked ice into a cocktail shaker and shake well for a minute or two. Pour into the glass and add enough water to fill the glass seven-eighths full; stir well and serve at once.

RASPBERRYADE

¼ glass of raspberry juice,
½ teaspoonful of lemon juice,
1 teaspoonful of powdered sugar,
　Cracked ice,
　Water.

Pour the raspberry juice, lemon juice, sugar and cracked ice into a shaker — using an iced tea glass as a measuring medium — and shake well; pour into the iced tea glass and fill with water. Stir and serve.

LEMON FROTH

1 egg white,
Lemon syrup (see lemonade),
¾ cupful of water,
1 candied cherry.

To three-quarters of a cup of water add one-third cupful of finely cracked ice and lemon syrup enough to please the taste of the person to be served: shake well for two minutes, strain into a tall thin glass — an iced tea glass is a desirable type — and stir in the stiffly beaten white of an egg. Top with a thin slice of lemon and a candied cherry.

STRAWBERRY-LEMON FROTH

1 egg white,
½ lemon,
¾ cupful of water,
Cracked ice,
2 teaspoonfuls of sugar,
½ dozen strawberries.

Reserve the largest berry and crush the others; press through a fine sieve. Extract the juice from half a lemon, add to the strawberry juice and stir in the sugar. Continue to stir until the sugar is dissolved. Pour this into a cocktail shaker, adding the finely cracked ice and water. Shake hard for two minutes, strain into a tall glass, stir in the stiffly beaten white of an egg and top with the selected strawberry.

HOT LEMONADE

½ lemon,
3 teaspoonfuls of sugar,
1¼ cupfuls of boiling water.

Extract the juice from the half lemon, add the sugar and then the hot water. Stir until the sugar is dissolved and serve.

HOT SPICED LEMONADE

½ lemon,
3 teaspoonfuls of sugar,
1¼ cupfuls of boiling water,
¼ teaspoonful of ground ginger.

Extract the juice from the half lemon, add the sugar and ginger; strain and add the boiling water. Stir until the sugar is dissolved and serve.

FRAPPÉS

Any one of the fruitades may be made into a frappé with so little trouble that in hot weather there is no reason why the hostess should not serve these cooling, delectable drinks at a moment's notice. There are always syrups which may be kept in the refrigerator and mixed with lemon syrup, a little water or carbonated water added, poured over the shaved ice in a sherbet glass, and presto! the frappé is ready to serve.

It is also possible to freeze the frappé, and it is advisable if one is to serve a goodly number. Remember always that a frappé is only partially frozen. As the liquid begins to thicken, scrape it from the sides of the freezer, using a long knife, preferably a spatula. It would seem impossible to keep house without a spatula, because of the many uses to which it may be put.

LEMON-RASPBERRY FRAPPÉ

Shaved ice,
1 tablespoonful of lemon syrup (see lemonade),
1 tablespoonful of raspberry juice.

This is only enough for one service. Fill a sherbet glass three-quarters full of finely shaved ice and pour over it the lemon syrup and raspberry juice. Serve at once. This may be served at the beginning of a meal In hot weather, or served at any time when any cooling drink is wanted.

BLACKBERRY FRAPPÉ

Shaved ice,
2 tablespoonfuls of blackberry juice,
Sugar.

Fill the sherbet glasses three-quarters full of shaved ice, and pour the blackberry juice over after having been mixed with sugar enough to take away the decided acid taste. It is not wise to make any drink which is meant to be cooling, too sweet.

WHITE GRAPE JUICE FRAPPÉ

Shaved ice,
¼ teaspoonful of lemon syrup,
2 tablespoonfuls of white grape juice.

Fill the glass,— a sherbet or tall champagne glass — with finely shaved ice, and pour over it the grape juice and lemon syrup (see lemonade). Serve at once.

TEA FRAPPÉ

2 teaspoonfuls of tea,
1½ pints of boiling water,
4 teaspoonfuls of sugar,
2 tablespoonfuls of lemon juice.

Use a large teapot, rinsing it out with boiling water, then place the tea in the pot and pour a pint and a half of boiling water over. Allow to stand for five minutes, and strain off. Cool, add the sugar and the lemon juice and freeze to a mush. Serve in sherbet glasses with a mint leaf, if mint is in season.

PINEAPPLE FRAPPÉ

1 pineapple,
1 cupful of sugar,
1 lemon,
1 quart of water.

Peel the pineapple, remove the " eyes," and holding the pines in the left hand slash both ways,— up and down, as well as across,— then cut away from the stalk-like center. One may crush more thoroughly by putting through a food chopper, or by using a large wooden spoon. Extract as much juice as possible, and add to the sugar and lemon juice. Stir, add the water, which should be boiling. Allow to cool, freeze until a mush, and serve. Remember always that a frappé is *right* when it is just at the pouring stage, and not frozen a bit harder.

STRAWBERRY FRAPPÉ

1 quart of strawberries,
1 lemon,
1 quart of water,
1½ cupfuls of sugar.

Crush the strawberries, press through a fine sieve, add the sugar and lemon juice; add the water, which should be boiling. Set aside to cool; pour into the freezer and freeze until a soft pourable mush. Serve in tall champagne glasses and top with a selected strawberry.

COFFEE FRAPPÉ

Whipped cream,
2 level tablespoonfuls of powdered coffee,
1 cupful of boiling water,
2 teaspoonfuls of sugar,
Shaved ice.

Powder the coffee, put in the bag of a drip pot and pour the cupful of boiling water over it. Allow this to drip, add the sugar and stir until dissolved. Put into the refrigerator and when ready to serve, pour two tablespoonfuls over the shaved ice in the sherbet glass. The glass should be about three-quarters full, which allows space for the coffee. Top with a generous spoonful of whipped cream.

EASILY MADE FRAPPÉS

It may not be known to all housekeepers that fruit syrups may be purchased at very reasonable prices from the better grocers, but it is true, and with these syrups and shaved ice a frappé may be made in a minute.

RASPBERRY FRAPPÉ

Shaved ice,
Raspberry syrup.

Fill the sherbet glasses about three-quarters full with finely shaved ice, and pour over it two tablespoonfuls of raspberry syrup. Serve at once.

STRAWBERRY FRAPPÉ

Shaved ice,
Strawberry syrup.

If one owns a supply of attractive glasses, one can always make drinks *look* differently at least, and one's appetite is always grateful for a change, even a change in the type of glasses used.

I would suggest if one has tall thin glasses of the type of parfait glasses, using them for a change.

Fill until about a quarter way from the top with shaved ice, and pour over four tablespoonfuls of strawberry syrup. Serve immediately.

GRENADINE FRAPPÉ

Shaved ice,
Grenadine,
½ teaspoonful of lemon juice.

Use a long-stemmed, tall glass, filling it three-quarters full with shaved ice. Over this pour four tablespoonfuls of grenadine in which the lemon juice has been mixed.

MOCK CHAMPAGNE FRAPPÉ

1 quart of sweet cider,
1 pint of carbonated water.

Pour into a freezer and freeze until about half frozen, or until a mush. Serve in champagne glasses.

ECONOMICAL FRAPPÉS

There are many times when a small amount of juice from either canned or preserved fruits is left from the table serving, although all the fruit may have been used, and there is no reason why this juice should not be used to good advantage in frappés. One should remember always that the syrup from preserved fruits is much heavier, and in consequence would be somewhat too sweet to use as it came from the fruit unless a little acid were added to it. So, when using the syrup of preserves add lemon juice and the frappé will be much more acceptable and refreshing.

PEACH FRAPPÉ

Shaved ice,
1 teaspoonful of lemon juice,
2 tablespoonfuls of syrup from preserved peaches.

Use a sherbet glass and fill three-quarters full with shaved ice; pour over this the syrup from the peaches which should have been mixed with the lemon juice. Serve as soon as prepared.

CHERRY FRAPPÉ

If the cherries have been canned with a thin syrup it may be used just as it is taken from the fruit. It will need neither sugar nor lemon juice.

Shaved ice,
3 tablespoonfuls of cherry juice.

Fill the sherbet glass three-quarters full of ice and pour over the juice or light syrup from the canned cherries. Serve immediately.

II — FRUIT PUNCHES, FRUIT CUPS AND FRUIT BOWLS

The art of mixing a satisfying punch is not at all as mystifying as it is often thought to be. To mix enough for a number of guests one should own a punch bowl, and while one may spend almost any amount of money on such a thing, there are very inexpensive pressed glass bowls to be purchased. It is always advisable to select the very plainest style one can find. One of the better pressed glass bowls is in the desirable colonial pattern and will be found to be most satisfactory.

APPLEBLOOM PUNCH

1 pint of sweet cider,
1 pint of Apollinaris,
1 pint of white grape juice,
    Ice.

Place a square of ice in the punch bowl and pour the sweet cider and white grape juice over it, allow this to become very cold, and last pour the Apollinaris over. Serve in low punch glasses.

BRISTOL PUNCH

1 quart of boiling water,
2 tablespoonfuls of tea,
6 sprays of fresh mint,
1 cupful of sugar,
2 lemons,
1 quart of sparkling apple juice (commercial).

Crush the mint, add the tea and pour the boiling water

over, allowing it to stand for five minutes. Strain and cool,
add the sugar and the lemons, which should have been
washed and sliced very thin. Add two cupfuls of cracked
ice to this and allow it to chill. When ready to serve place
a square of ice in the punch bowl and strain the liquid over;
add a cupful of red raspberries and a quart of commercial
cider of the sparkling type. This is readily obtainable at a
first class grocer's.

Serve in tall glasses.

DÉBUTANTE PUNCH

3 lemons,
2 oranges,
6 sprays of mint,
1 quart of grape juice,
1 pint of carbonated water,
½ pint of tea (green),
1 cupful of sugar,
1 pint of water.

To a half teaspoonful of green tea use a half pint of
boiling water; allow to infuse for five or six minutes, strain
and cool. Extract the juice from the lemons, add the sugar
and water and mix with the cooled tea. Prepare a punch
bowl by placing a piece of ice in the center; pour the tea
and lemon mixture over and add two oranges peeled and
cut into halves and slices, then the mint, crushing the leaves
before using. Allow this to stand for a few minutes and
pour in the grape juice, and last, the carbonated water.
The punch should be served as soon as ready.

CIDER PUNCH

2 quarts of sweet cider,
½ pint of loganberry juice.
3 lemons,
3 oranges,

2 cupfuls of sugar,
3 pints of carbonated water.

As loganberry juice is tart more sugar is seemingly
needed than when grape juice is used, but it is far better
to err on the other side and serve a punch too tart rather
than too sweet. It is always wise to taste any drink one is
preparing.

Peel the lemons and extract the juice, extract the juice
from two of the oranges and mix with the Loganberry juice
and sugar and pour into the punch bowl, in which a large
piece of ice should have been placed. Slice the third orange
very thin and place in the bowl. Pour the carbonated water
over all and the punch is ready to serve.

GINGER ALE PUNCH

1 cupful of sugar,
1½ cupfuls of tea,
1 cupful of orange juice,
1 pint of ginger ale,
1 pint of Apollinaris,
¼ cupful of lemon juice,
   Ice.

Pour one cupful and a half of boiling water over a level
teaspoonful of tea and allow to infuse for five minutes;
strain and pour over the sugar, stir and allow to cool. When
cool add the fruit juices; place a small block of ice in the
punch bowl and pour the liquid over. Just before serving
add the ginger ale and the Apollinaris and float several thin
slices of orange.

GRENADINE PUNCH

1 quart of water,
1 quart of carbonated water,
¼ cupful of grenadine,

    4 lemons,
    2 oranges,
   12 large strawberries,
    1 cupful of sugar,
       Ice.

Extract the juice from both the lemons and oranges and
mix with the sugar; allow this to stand on the ice until
ready to serve, then mix with the water. Place a square of
ice in the punch bowl and pour the mixture over it; stir in
the grenadine and add the strawberries, and last add the
carbonated water. Serve immediately.

LOGANBERRY PUNCH

    1 pint of loganberry juice,
    1 quart of water,
    4 lemons,
   1½ cupfuls of sugar,
    1 pint of Apollinaris.

Extract the juice from the lemons and add to the loganberry juice and sugar, stirring well; add the water and
pour over a square of ice in the punch bowl. When ready
to serve pour in the Apollinaris, and serve at once.

BERKSHIRE FRUIT PUNCH

    1 quart of Apollinaris,
    1 cupful of lemon juice,
    1 cupful of orange juice,
    1 pineapple, grated,
    2 cupfuls of selected strawberries,
    2 cupfuls of strong tea,
    2 cupfuls of sugar,
    1 orange cut into very thin slices,
    1 cupful of Maraschino cherries,
       Ice water.

Boil the sugar and two cupfuls of water until syrup-like,

and add the lemon and orange juice. Grate the pineapple and hull the strawberries; make the tea by pouring two cupfuls of boiling water over one and a half teaspoonfuls of tea, allowing it to infuse for six minutes. Mix the syrup, fruit juices, tea and grated pineapple, and add two quarts of iced water; stir well and pour over a square of ice in the punch bowl. Add the orange, sliced very thin and cut into halves, and the strawberries. When ready to serve pour the Apollinaris over all and serve at once.

If strawberries are out of season, use Malaga grapes, cut in two and seeded.

An ideal decoration is to use grapes in bunches, hanging them around the edge of the bowl. Use white and blue grapes, or red and white; separating them with grape leaves if they are obtainable.

HONEY BLOSSOM PUNCH

    1 cupful of honey,
    1 cupful of sugar,
    1 quart of water,
    2 lemons,
   12 oranges,
    1 pineapple,
   24 strawberries,
      Ice,
      Carbonated water.

Boil the honey, sugar, two cupfuls of water and the grated rind or zest of one orange together for five minutes. Allow to cool and add the other two cupfuls of water and the juice of the oranges and lemons; stir and pour over a block of ice in the punch bowl. Add the grated pineapple and the strawberries, which should have been hulled. When ready for service add the carbonated water, using a quart.

COLUMBIA PINEAPPLE PUNCH

1 pint of sweet cider,
1 pineapple,
2 oranges,
4 slices of cucumber,
2 cupfuls of selected strawberries,
1 banana,
Ground cinnamon,
Apollinaris,
1 cupful of sugar.

Shred into very small pieces the edible part of a very ripe pineapple and add the oranges sliced very thin, the cucumber slices and the strawberries cut into halves, one banana cut into dice and a generous cupful of sugar. Stir these together with a pint of iced water and allow to stand for a half hour on the ice. Remove the cucumber slices, add a quarter-teaspoonful of ground cinnamon; add the cider and last, the Apollinaris. Serve at once.

The most satisfactory glasses to use would be tall slim glasses, serving a long handled spoon — an iced-tea-spoon will do — with each service so that the fruit may be eaten.

PUNCH À LA PARISIENNE

1 pound of pulverized sugar,
6 lemons,
6 oranges,
1 small pineapple,
½ pound of malaga grapes, skinned and **seeded,**
½ pint bottle of Maraschino cherries,
2 quarts of grape juice,
2 quarts of Apollinaris,
2 quarts of ginger ale,
Ice.

Use a large punch bowl; into which put an eight inch cube of ice; over which pour the following mixture; the juice of six lemons, which should have been peeled before squeezing, the juice of six oranges, sugar, and grape juice; stir to dissolve the sugar and add the shredded pineapple, maraschino cherries and the peeled and seeded grapes. Do not allow this to stand, but pour the ginger ale and Apollinaris over and serve immediately. If the punch seems too thick, a pint of water or more may be added without detriment.

CHOCOLATE PUNCH

This is an individual punch, and should be made in a shaker.

½ cupful of chocolate extract,
1 teaspoonful of sugar,
1 egg,
Ice,
Milk to fill glass.

Place all the ingredients in a cocktail shaker and shake well; strain into a tall thin glass and serve.

MILK PUNCH

1 cupful of milk,
¼ cupful of strawberry syrup,
1 teaspoonful of sugar,
1 egg,
Ice.

Put all the ingredients into a shaker and shake thoroughly, strain into a tall glass and serve at once.

VANILLA MILK PUNCH

1¼ cupfuls of milk,
½ teaspoonful of vanilla,
1 teaspoonful of sugar,
1 egg,
Ice.

Place all the ingredients in a cocktail shaker and shake well; strain into a tall glass, sprinkle with a little nutmeg and serve at once.

ORANGE COUNTY PUNCH

1 egg,
1 lemon,
1 teaspoonful of sugar,
1¼ cupfuls of sweet cider,
   Cracked ice.
   Carbonated water.

Put the egg, juice of the lemon, sugar, cider and ice in a cocktail shaker and shake for a minute or two, strain into a tall glass and fill with carbonated water. It were best to use a syphon.

POPULAR PINEAPPLE PUNCH

1 pineapple,
3 oranges,
2 lemons,
1 cupful of sugar,
1 cupful of home-made raspberry syrup,
1 quart of white grape juice,
1 quart of ginger ale,
   Ice,
   Cherries.
   Water.

Extract the juice from the oranges and lemons, and mix with the raspberry syrup and the sugar; grate the pineapple and add to the foregoing mixture, adding enough iced water to make a full pint. Allow this to stand for ten minutes, arrange a square of ice in a punch bowl and pour the mixture over, adding the grape juice and ginger ale just at serving time.

MOCK CLARET PUNCH

1 quart of grape juice,
4 lemons,
1 cupful of sugar,
1 stick of cinnamon,
1 quart of water.

Extract the juice from the lemons and add the sugar and stick of cinnamon, allowing this to stand on the ice for an hour. At the expiration of that time add the water and grape juice; pour over a block of ice in the punch bowl and serve. (It were well to remove the stick of cinnamon before serving, however.)

MOCK CRÉOLE CLARET PUNCH

2½ quarts of grape juice,
1 pint of lemon juice,
1½ quarts of Apollinaris,
1 pound of sugar,
2 sliced lemons,
  Water,
  Ice.

Mix the grape juice, lemon juice, sugar and enough water to thin to please the taste of the hostess. Stir until the sugar is dissolved, and pour over a block of ice in the punch bowl. To this add the thinly sliced lemons and last, the Apollinaris.

STRAWBERRY PUNCH

3 quarts of strawberries,
2 quarts of carbonated water,
1 dozen lemons,
2 pineapples,
1 pound of sugar (more if desired),
1½ quarts of white grape juice,
  Ice,
  Selected strawberries.

Extract the juice from the lemons, shred and crush one pineapple and extract the juice, shred the second pineapple very fine, crush the strawberries (reserving a dozen large ones) and press through a fine sieve; mix the fruit juices with the sugar and white grape juice and allow to chill on the ice. Prepare a square of ice in the punch bowl and pour this mixture over it, add the second shredded pineapple and the selected strawberries, and pour over all the carbonated water. Serve at once.

STAUNTON FRUIT PUNCH

1 grape fruit,
1 cupful of raspberry syrup (home-made or commercial),
4 lemons,
1 quart of white grape juice,
1 pint of ginger ale,
1 quart brick of orange ice,
1 cupful of sugar,
  Ice.

Extract the juice from the grape fruit and lemons and stir in the sugar and the raspberry syrup, add one quart of iced water and stir until the sugar is dissolved. Place a block of ice in the center of the punch bowl; pour the mixture over, add the grape juice and ginger ale, and then just as it is ready to be served place a brick of orange water ice in the center. Serve immediately.

It might seem that it would be necessary to stir the water ice in, but it is not, as quite enough is gathered by the ladle.

FLORIDA PUNCH

12 oranges,
2 lemons,
1 pineapple,
1 brick of raspberry water ice,
½ cupful of sugar (more if liked),
1 pint of Apollinaris,

Water,
Ice.

Extract the juice from the oranges and lemons, grate the pineapple and mix well with the sugar. Add a quart and a pint of iced water, and set on the ice for a half hour. Place a square of ice in the punch bowl and pour the mixture over it. Allow it to stand for ten minutes, add the Apollinaris and then the raspberry ice. Serve as soon as the water ice is added.

Small pieces of thinly sliced orange add to the attractiveness of the punch.

FRESH MINT PUNCH

12 sprays of fresh mint,
3 lemons,
6 oranges,
¾ cupful of sugar,
1½ quarts of ginger ale,
1 pint of sweet cider,
1 pint of iced water,
   Ice,
   Vegetable color.

Crush the mint, extract the juice from the oranges and the lemons, add the sugar and water, stirring until the sugar is dissolved. Place this in a punch bowl and arrange a square of ice in the center. Pour over this the cider and ginger ale, to which add enough green vegetable color to make the punch a good shade of green when stirred in.

MOCK CHAMPAGNE PUNCH

1 quart of sparkling cider,
1 quart of white grape juice,
4 lemons,
½ cupful of sugar,

1 pint of ginger ale,
1 pint of iced water,
   Ice.

There is to be purchased in the market now a commercial apple-juice, which is carbonated, and this should be used unless one has made the sparkling cider at home.

Extract the juice from the lemons and add the sugar and water; stir until the sugar is dissolved: add the grape juice. Place a block of ice in a punch bowl and pour this mixture over it, and then add the sparkling cider and the ginger ale.

PUNCHES FROM SYRUPS

Delicious punches may be made from syrups, whether home-made or commercial, whether made as syrups for this purpose or the fruit syrups from preserves, or the medium syrups from the cold-pack canning.

Very often there is more syrup or juice than is needed for table service in a jar of berries, and this juice may be used at once, or a little more sugar added, reheated, placed in cans, sealed and put away for later use.

For instance; if a can of strawberries is opened and found to have more juice than usual, pour off the surplus and use at once, or add enough sugar to make a thicker syrup,—which amount will have to be determined by the amount of juice,— and re-can and store.

STRAWBERRY-LEMON PUNCH

2 cupfuls of strawberry syrup,
3 lemons,
2 teaspoonfuls of strawberry extract,
⅔ cupfuls of sugar,
1 pint of water,
1 quart of carbonated water.

Extract the juice from the lemons by using a glass extractor and add the sugar, allowing this to stand for a half hour. Add the water, strawberry syrup and extract and pour this over a block of ice in the punch bowl. Just before serving add the carbonated water.

METROPOLITAN RASPBERRY PUNCH

For this punch either the commercial or home-made syrup may be used.

2 cupfuls of raspberry syrup,
2 lemons,
½ cupful of sugar,
1 pint of water,
1 pint of ginger ale,
1 pint of Apollinaris.

Mix the sugar with the lemon juice, and allow it to stand for a half hour on ice if possible, then add the water and the raspberry syrup; stir well and pour over a square of ice in the punch bowl. At serving time add the ginger ale and the Apollinaris. Serve immediately.

PLUM PUNCH

2 cupfuls of plum syrup,
3 lemons,
1 small pineapple,
¾ cupful of sugar,
1 quart of Apollinaris,
1 pint of grape juice,
1 pint of water.

Extract the juice from the lemons and add the sugar and the plum syrup; stand on ice to chill, and grate the pineapple. Mix the lemon juice, sugar, plum syrup, water, grape juice and the grated pineapple together and pour over a block of ice in the punch bowl. When ready to serve add the Apollinaris. Serve immediately.

FAIRY PUNCH

½ cupful of lime syrup,
½ cupful of raspberry syrup,
½ cupful of strawberry syrup,
½ cupful of pineapple syrup,
2 oranges,
2 lemons,
¼ cupful of sugar,
1 quart of raspberry water ice,
1 pint of ginger ale,
1 pint of water,
1 quart of carbonated water,
  Ice.

Extract the juice from the lemons and the oranges and mix with the sugar; add the lime, raspberry, strawberry and pineapple syrups, and stir in the water; pour this mixture over a square of ice in the punch bowl and add the ginger ale and the carbonated water. Slip the square of raspberry water ice into the center of the bowl and serve at once.

CUP DE LUXE

1 pint of white grape juice,
1 pint of cider,
1 pint of Apollinaris,
¼ cupful of grenadine,
  Ice,
  Mint,
  Strawberries,
  Pineapple,
  Cherries.

Serve in a tall, straight glass pitcher and mix in the following manner; mix the cider, grape juice and grenadine, pour into the pitcher, add a pint of cracked ice, stir and add the mint, strawberries, cherries and half of a small pineapple shredded finely. Pour in the Apollinaris when ready to serve and not before. Serve in tall thin glasses.

CIDER CUP

1 quart of sweet cider,
½ pint of white grape juice,
1 pint of carbonated water,
    Mint,
    Skinned and seeded malaga grapes,
    Shredded pineapple.

Mix the cider and grape juice and pour over a pint of crushed or cracked ice; add a quarter of a pineapple finely shredded and the malaga grapes, and when ready to serve pour in the carbonated water.

LOGANBERRY CUP

1 pint of loganberry juice,
1 pint of iced water,
1 pint of cider,
1 pint of carbonated water,
    Cherries,
    Strawberries,
    Mint,
    Sugar.

Mix the loganberry juice, water, and cider and pour into the pitcher over a pint of cracked ice; add a little sugar if necessary as loganberry juice is very tart,— and then put in the fruit and last, add the carbonated water. Serve in tall straight sided glasses.

ROSE-MINT CUP

½ cupful of grenadine,
3 teaspoonfuls of rose extract,
1 quart of white grape juice,
1 pint of ginger ale,
1 pint of water,
12 sprays of mint,
    Ice.

Crush the mint slightly and put into the pitcher with a pint of cracked ice; mix grenadine, rose extract, grape juice and water and pour over the mint and ice. Add the ginger ale and serve at once.

KAATERSKILL CUP

1 pint of tea infusion,
1 pint of ginger ale,
1 pint of carbonated water,
¼ cupful of raspberry syrup,
1 large spray of mint,
¼ small pineapple shredded,
   Ice.

Make the tea by pouring one pint of boiling water over two teaspoonfuls of tea — green or English Breakfast, as preferred — and allow it to infuse for six minutes, then strain. Allow to chill, and add to the raspberry syrup. Put a pint of cracked ice in a tall pitcher, crush the mint, and place that and the shredded pineapple with the ice, covering with the tea and raspberry mixture. When ready to serve add the ginger ale and carbonated water.

WHITE GRAPE JUICE CUP

1 quart of white grape juice,
1 pint of ginger ale,
1 pint of Apollinaris,
¼ cupful of pineapple syrup,
   Mint.

Mix the grape juice and the pineapple syrup and pour over a pint of cracked ice in a tall pitcher. Crush the mint slightly and add that to the mixture. At serving time add the Apollinaris and ginger ale. Use tall slim glasses, or narrow goblets.

MINT-LOGANBERRY CUP

1 pint of loganberry juice,
1 quart of carbonated water,
12 sprays of mint well crushed,
2 teaspoonfuls of lime syrup,
   Ice.

Crush the mint, and place in a pitcher with a pint of cracked ice. Add the loganberry juice, lime syrup and the carbonated water and serve at once.

AYLESFORD FRUIT CUP

1 pint of grape juice,
1 pint of sweet cider,
1 pint of Apollinaris,
½ pineapple shredded,
1 cupful of selected strawberries,
2 tablespoonfuls of preserved cherries,
6 sprays of mint,
   Ice.

Shred the pineapple very fine, crush the mint slightly and place in a tall glass pitcher with a pint of cracked ice. Pour the grape juice and cider over this, add the strawberries and cherries and last, pour in the Apollinaris. Serve immediately in tall straight-sided glasses.

Be sure to serve a generous spoonful of fruit with each service. A long handled spoon will aid in eating the fruit in comfort.

CANTON CUP

1 pint of tea infusion,
1 quart of ginger ale,
2 lemons,
2 tablespoonfuls of preserved ginger and the syrup,
1 cupful of pitted cherries (white, if possible),
   Ice,
   Sugar.

Chop the ginger until very fine; extract the juice from the lemons and mix with the chopped ginger and a table-spoonful of the syrup from the preserves, and a half cupful of sugar. Stand on the ice for a half hour and pour over a pint of cracked ice in a pitcher. When ready to serve add the tea (either green or Ceylon) and the ginger ale. Last, add the cherries and serve.

CUP À LA MEDLEY.

1 pint of rice water,
1 cupful of sugar,
2 lemons,
2 oranges,
1 stick cinnamon,
4 cloves,
1 allspice,
½ cupful of seeded raisins,
1 pint of ginger ale,
1 quart of carbonated water,
  Grated rind of one lemon,
  Ice.

This recipe gives the housekeeper an opportunity to use the water in which rice is boiled, and which is usually thrown away.

Make a syrup by boiling one pint of rice water, one cupful of sugar, the grated rind of one lemon, one stick of cinnamon, four cloves, and one cupful of raisins together for ten or twelve minutes. Strain carefully and chill. When ready to serve pour into a tall pitcher in which a pint of cracked ice has been placed; add two oranges thinly sliced and pour over this the carbonated water and ginger ale. Serve immediately.

FLORIDA WEST COAST CUP

3 oranges,
1 lemon,
½ small pineapple,

2 kumquats,
1 pint of carbonated water,
1 quart of water,
¾ cupful of sugar,
   Ice.

Peel and shred the pineapple, saving all the juice; extract
the juice from the oranges and the lemon. Boil one cupful
of water and the sugar for six minutes and allow to cool.
Mix the syrup thus made with the juices of the fruits, and
pour into a tall slim glass pitcher; add the kumquats thinly
sliced and the remaining pint and a half of water. Add a
pint of cracked ice and the carbonated water. Stir well and
serve at once.

FRUIT BOWL

1 ripe pineapple,
1 pound of powdered sugar,
4 quarts of white grape juice,
1 quart of sparkling cider,
1 pound of block sugar,
   Ice.

Peel the pineapple and cut into thin slices; place in a
large bowl and cover with the powdered sugar; cover the
bowl and allow to stand for ten or twelve hours. Add the
grape juice and the block sugar and stand on ice. Just
before serving add the sparkling cider.

APPLE BOWL

1 pound of powdered sugar,
12 apples, red and juicy,
¼ cupful of grenadine,
2 quarts of white grape juice,
1 quart of sparkling cider,
1 quart of ginger ale,
   Ice.

Peel the apples (winesaps are excellent apples to use) core them and slice very thin. Place in a large bowl and cover with the sugar, cover and allow to stand on ice for ten hours. Pour the grenadine and grape juice over this and allow this to stand for two hours longer. Strain through a flannel into a punch bowl and add the cider, ginger ale and a pint of cracked ice. Serve immediately.

BADMINTON BOWL

½ a medium sized cucumber,
6 ounces of powdered sugar,
¼ teaspoonful of grated nutmeg,
1 quart of grape juice,
1 quart of Apollinaris,
  Ice.

Peel carefully and cut into thin slices the half cucumber; place in a bowl and sprinkle with the sugar and nutmeg. Allow this to stand for ten minutes and add the grape juice. Place this on ice for a half hour; strain, add the Apollinaris and serve at once.

CARDINAL BOWL

4 oranges,
1½ pounds of block sugar,
1 quart of white grape juice,
1 pint of carbonated water,
  Ice.

Grate the rind of two oranges, and squeeze the juice of four over the block sugar and add a quart of white grape juice: allow this to stand on the ice for a half hour, strain through a flannel and add the carbonated water. Serve this in a punch bowl, being sure to serve it as soon as the carbonated water is added.

BIRMINGHAM BOWL

8 oranges,
1 pound of block sugar,
3 quarts of white grape juice,
1 quart of ginger ale,
1 pint of purple grape juice,
2 sticks of cinnamon,
    Ice.

Peel the outer skin of two of the oranges and add one quart of white grape juice and two sticks of cinnamon, allowing this to stand on ice for three hours and then strain. Extract the juice from eight oranges and pour over the sugar. Allow the sugar to melt, mix with the strained grape juice, add the remaining grape juice, both purple and white, mix and at serving time add the ginger ale.

ENGLISH CIDER BOWL

½ pint of green tea infusion,
¼ pound of block sugar,
1 quart of sweet cider,
1 pint of ginger ale,
2 slices of fresh cucumber,
3 sprays of thyme,
1 sage leaf,
    Ice.

Make the tea infusion by pouring a half pint of boiling water over a teaspoonful of green tea allowing it to stand for six minutes; strain and pour into a bowl with the block sugar, cider, cucumber, thyme and sage. Allow this to stand on the ice for a half hour, strain and add the ginger ale and a pint of shaved ice. Serve as soon as the ginger ale is added.

SPARKLING CIDER BOWL

1 orange,
1 lime,
3 slices of cucumber,
1 sage leaf,
3 sprigs of balm,
¼ cupful of grenadine (4 tablespoonfuls),
1 quart of plain sweet cider,
1 quart of sparkling cider,
½ pound of block sugar,
    Ice.

Peel an orange very thin, reserve the orange and put the peeling into a cupful of boiling water and allow it to remain a half hour. Strain this into a bowl and add the grenadine, sugar, balm, sage and sweet cider; place on ice for a half hour and again strain. Add the juice of the orange and lime, a pint of cracked ice and the sparkling cider; serve immediately.

LOGANBERRY BOWL

1 orange,
½ cucumber,
½ pound of powdered sugar,
1 spray of mint,
1 quart of loganberry juice,
1 quart of iced water,
1 quart of ginger ale,
    Ice.

Peel the orange, cut it into thin slices, slice the half cucumber very thin and place all in a bowl, including the orange peeling; add the sugar, loganberry juice, and mint, and allow to stand on ice for a half hour. At the end of that time add the iced water, stir and strain.

When ready to serve add the ginger ale.

III — COCKTAILS, HIGHBALLS, FIZZES, COBBLERS, SOURS AND JULEPS

NON-ALCOHOLIC COCKTAILS

As the mission of a cocktail is to be an appetizer, it should be served at the beginning of a meal. It may be made of fruits, of vegetables, of both fruits and vegetables, or of liquids, as one wishes. Most cocktails served at the home table will doubtless be made of fresh fruits, but the housekeeper will find that there are a number of combinations of fruits and vegetables which will be quite acceptable to her family and guests.

There are several things to remember when making a cocktail; one of which is, always use attractive glasses and be sure that they shine. Have the ingredients quite cold and by no means make them too sweet, for if they lose the tartness, the best effect is lost.

The more attractive the cocktail *looks,* the more appetizing it will prove to be.

CUCUMBER COCKTAIL

For individual portion use the following:
2 tablespoonfuls of peeled, chopped cucumber,
¼ teaspoonful of grated horse-radish,
¼ teaspoonful of chopped onion,
1 teaspoonful of chopped celery,
¼ teaspoonful of chopped radish (not peeled),
  Salt,
  French dressing,
  Paprika.

Chop the cucumber, celery, onion and radish; mix with the horse-radish, and salt to taste. Drain and mix with a little French dressing, place in either sherbet or cocktail glasses, which have been chilled, and serve very cold. Berry forks, oyster forks, or small salad forks are best to use for vegetable cocktails.

TOMATO COCKTAIL

For individual portion use:
2 tablespoonfuls of minced tomato,
2 tablespoonfuls of aspic jelly, cut into dice,
¼ teaspoonful of chopped chives,
2 tablespoonfuls of chopped celery,
  French dressing,
  Green peppers.

Remove the tops from as many peppers as are needed, remove the seeds and membrane and place on ice to chill. Cut the aspic jelly into dice, mince the tomato and chop the celery and chives, mix and drain. Use only enough French dressing to mix well. Serve very cold.

PEACH COCKTAIL

For each portion use:
1 peach,
4 drops of lemon juice,
3 Maraschino cherries,
3 tablespoonfuls of raspberry syrup,
  Ice.

Drop the ripe peach in hot water for one minute, remove the skin and chill the peach. Cut into small pieces, add the Maraschino cherries cut into quarters, and mix with a tablespoonful of shaved ice and three tablespoonfuls of raspberry syrup, either home-made or commercial. Serve very cold. Use a spoon with a fruit cocktail.

ORANGE COCKTAIL

For each service use:

½ orange,
½ banana,
3 Maraschino cherries,
6 drops of lemon juice,
3 tablespoonfuls of strawberry syrup,
 Ice.

After peeling the orange and banana, cut into small pieces, quarter the cherries, mix with a tablespoonful of shaved ice, the strawberry syrup and lemon juice and serve in sherbet glasses. Use a spoon with this cocktail. Serve very cold.

STRAWBERRY COCKTAIL

For each service use:

8 selected strawberries,
6 Malaga grapes,
1 tablespoonful of grenadine,
1 tablespoonful of cherry syrup,
 Ice.

Hull the strawberries, peel the grapes and remove the seeds, cutting the grapes in two; mix with a tablespoonful of shaved ice, the grenadine and the cherry syrup. Syrup from home-made preserves may be used or one may use commercial syrup. Serve thoroughly chilled.

A sherbet glass will be found most satisfactory for this cocktail.

WATERMELON COCKTAIL

½ teaspoonful of chopped mint,
4 tablespoonfuls of white grape juice,
 Watermelon cubes to fill the glass,
 Ice.

Select the heart of the watermelon and cut it into small

cubes; chop a few leaves of mint (about an eighth tea-spoonful) and sprinkle over. Cover with a tablespoonful of shaved ice and add the white grape juice. Serve very cold.

CANTALOUPE COCKTAIL

3 preserved or fresh cherries,
3 tablespoonfuls of orange juice,
1 tablespoonful of shaved ice,
    Rounds of cantaloupe to fill the glass.

Cut balls from a ripe cantaloupe, using a vegetable cutter; place them in the serving glass: add the cherries, cut into small pieces, the ice and the orange juice. Serve thoroughly chilled.

MALAGA COCKTAIL

½ cupful of Malaga grapes,
6 Maraschino cherries,
1 tablespoonful of grenadine,
½ cupful of orange cubes,
1 tablespoonful of cherry syrup,
    Ice.

Peel the grapes, cut in two and remove the seeds, peel and cut the orange into small dice, mix with the cherries, grenadine and cherry syrup. Add a tablespoonful of shaved ice and serve very cold in tall champagne or sherbet glasses.

GRAPEFRUIT COCKTAIL

For individual portion use:
2 sections of a large firm grape fruit,
4 sections of an orange,
6 Maraschino cherries,
6 Malaga grapes,
4 tablespoonfuls of raspberry syrup,
    Ice.

Separate the grape fruit and orange into sections and remove the membrane, break into small pieces — being sure to reserve the juice of the fruit; peel and seed the grapes, cut them in two and cut the cherries into pieces. Mix these with a tablespoonful of shaved ice and the raspberry syrup. Serve very cold.

COCKTAILS MADE FROM FRUIT JUICES

CLOVER LEAF COCKTAIL

1 cupful of orange juice,
⅛ cupful of grenadine (2 tablespoonfuls),
1 cupful of cracked ice,
1 egg white.

This will be quite enough for four cocktails.

Place all the ingredients into a cocktail shaker, and shake vigorously for two or three minutes, strain into cocktail glasses, which have been chilled. Serve immediately.

GOLDEN MIST COCKTAIL

1 cupful of sparkling cider or apple juice,
⅛ cupful of pineapple juice,
1 egg white,
1 cupful of cracked ice.

This, too, will be enough for four cocktails.

Place the ingredients into a cocktail shaker, and shake well for two minutes — *actually*, not guessing at the time — and strain into chilled cocktail glasses.

APPLEBLOW COCKTAIL

1 cupful of sparkling apple juice (commercial),
⅛ cupful of ginger ale,
½ teaspoonful of lime juice,
   Ice.

If fresh limes cannot be procured, use the commercial lime juice, but the fresh is greatly to be desired. The amount given will make four cocktails.

Mix the lime juice, ice and apple juice and pour into a cocktail shaker, shaking thoroughly. When ready to serve add the ginger ale, replace the strainer and strain into cocktail glasses.

ORANGEBLOSSOM COCKTAIL

1 cupful of orange juice,
¼ cupful of pineapple juice,
1 teaspoonful of orange flower water,
1 tablespoonful of plain syrup,
1 cupful of cracked ice.

Place all the ingredients into a cocktail shaker, shake hard for two minutes, strain into chilled cocktail glasses and serve at once.

This amount should be sufficient for four cocktails.

MARASCHINO COCKTAIL

¼ cupful of carbonated water,
4 Maraschino cherries,
¼ cupful of the syrup from the cherries,
1 cupful of orange juice,
1 cupful of cracked ice.

Pour the syrup from the cherries, the orange juice and the ice into a cocktail shaker. Shake well, add the carbonated water, strain into cocktail glasses, add a cherry to each glass and serve very cold.

CERISE COCKTAIL

¼ cupful of cherry juice,
1 cupful of sparkling apple juice (commercial),
4 preserved cherries,
1 cupful of cracked ice.

Put the cherry juice, which may be taken from canned red cherries, into a cocktail shaker with the cracked ice and the commercial apple juice and shake well. Strain into cocktail glasses, placing a cherry in each glass. Serve very cold.

ORCHARD COCKTAIL

1 cupful of sweet cider,
⅓ cupful of cherry juice,
½ inch of preserved ginger,
  Ice.

Chop the ginger, mix with the cider, cherry juice (homemade or commercial), and ice in the cocktail shaker. Shake well and strain into cocktail glasses.

SODA COCKTAIL

1 teaspoonful of powdered sugar,
2 dashes of Angostura bitters,
1 bottle club soda,
  Ice.

Put the ice, sugar and bitters into a soda glass, and pour the soda over. Stir with a spoon and serve.

HIGHBALLS

(non-alcoholic)

Highballs made from fruit juices, ginger ales and ciders are most delightful and satisfying, as well as being most cooling and refreshing. The hostess who makes a practice of serving these will find her recipes in great demand.

WHITE GRAPE JUICE HIGHBALL

1 cupful of white grape juice,
  Carbonated water (syphon),
  Ice.

Use a highball glass; after placing a tablespoonful of cracked ice in the glass, pour in the grape juice; fill nearly full with carbonated water, using a syphon.   Serve.

GINGER ALE HIGHBALL

½ pint of ginger ale,
1 teaspoonful of lime juice,
   Ice.

Put two tablespoonfuls of cracked ice in a highball glass, add the lime juice, which should be from fresh lime, and fill the glass with ginger ale.   Serve.

PURPLE GRAPE JUICE HIGHBALL

½ pint of grape juice,
1 teaspoonful of plain syrup (see syrups),
   Carbonated water (syphon),
   Ice.

Place two tablespoonfuls of cracked ice in a highball glass; pour over it the plain syrup and the purple grape juice; stir with a long handled spoon and add the carbonated water, using a syphon.   Serve.

LOGANBERRY HIGHBALL

½ pint of loganberry juice,
2 teaspoonfuls of plain syrup,
1 spray of mint,
   Carbonated water,
   Ice.

Crush the mint, put it in a highball glass with the loganberry juice, plain syrup and two tablespoonfuls of cracked ice.   Fill the glass nearly full with carbonated water, using a syphon   Serve immediately.

APPLE JUICE HIGHBALL

½ pint of sparkling apple juice (commercial),
   Carbonated water,
   Ice.

Put two tablespoonfuls of cracked ice in a highball glass, pour over it the apple juice and fill with carbonated water. Serve immediately.

GINGER-GRAPE HIGHBALL

½ pint of white grape juice,
   Ginger ale,
   Ice.

Put two tablespoonfuls of cracked ice in a highball glass, pour the grape juice over it, and add the ginger ale and serve.

CIDER HIGHBALL

1 cupful of sweet cider,
½ teaspoonful of lemon juice,
   Ice,
   Carbonated water.

Put two tablespoonfuls of cracked ice in a highball glass, add lemon juice and cider and fill nearly full with carbonated water, using a syphon. Serve at once.

GRENADINE HIGHBALL

¼ cupful of grenadine,
¾ cupful of sweet cider,
   Ice,
   Carbonated water.

Put two tablespoonfuls of cracked ice in a highball glass, pour over it the grenadine and the cider; fill to within an inch of the top of the glass with carbonated water, using a syphon. Serve.

FRUIT FIZZES

The glass in which to serve a fizz is straight-sided, in fact a tumbler, holding about eight ounces. There are variations of these, but it is best to match the rest of the glassware used on the table.

One necessary thing to remember about serving a fizz; always make it when it is to be drunk, not a minute sooner. *Serve as soon as finished.*

SILVER FRUIT FIZZ

1 tablespoonful of powdered sugar,
1 teaspoonful of lemon juice,
1 egg white,
⅓ of a cupful of cracked ice,
⅓ of a cupful of white grape juice,
   Carbonated water.

Put the egg white, ice, sugar, lemon juice and white grape juice in a shaker; shake well, strain into a fizz glass and fill nearly full with carbonated water. Use a syphon. Serve immediately.

GOLDEN FRUIT FIZZ

1 tablespoonful of powdered sugar,
1 teaspoonful of lime juice,
1 egg yolk,
⅓ cupful of white grape juice,
⅓ cupful of cracked ice.

Put the egg yolk, sugar, ice, grape juice and lime in a shaker; shake well, strain into a fizz glass and fill to within an inch of the top with carbonated water. A syphon is best.

LEMON FIZZ

½ lemon,
1 tablespoonful of powdered sugar,
  Carbonated water,
  Ice.

Extract the juice from half a lemon; strain it into a fizz glass with a tablespoonful of powdered sugar and a third of a cupful of cracked ice. Stir and fill the glass nearly full with carbonated water. A syphon is by far the better thing to use.

PURPLE FIZZ

⅓ cupful of purple grape juice,
½ teaspoonful of lemon juice,
1 tablespoonful of sugar,
  Ice,
  Carbonated water.

Put the grape juice, sugar, lemon juice and ice in a shaker and shake thoroughly; strain into a fizz glass and fill to within an inch of the top with carbonated water, using a syphon.

LOGANBERRY FIZZ

½ lime,
¼ cupful of loganberry juice,
1 tablespoonful of powdered sugar,
  Ice,
  Carbonated water.

Put the loganberry juice, sugar, lime juice and ice in a fizz glass and fill nearly full with carbonated water. Use a syphon. Serve immediately.

ROYAL FRUIT FIZZ

½ lemon,
1 egg,
½ cupful of sparkling apple juice,
  Ice,
  Carbonated water.

Put an egg, the apple juice, lemon juice and ice in a shaker and shake well; pour into a fizz glass and fill to within an inch of the top with carbonated water, using a syphon. Serve at once.

VIOLET FIZZ

1 lime,
1 teaspoonful sugar,
⅜ cupful shaved ice,
½ cupful of sparkling apple juice (commercial),
2 tablespoonfuls of raspberry syrup,
¼ cupful of sweet cream,
  Ice.

Extract the juice from the lime; pour into the shaker with ice, sugar, syrup and apple juice. Shake well; remove the top and add the cream, shake again, strain into a straight-sided fizz glass and serve. If the glass is not quite full enough, fill to within an inch of the top with carbonated water, using a syphon.

FRUIT JUICE SOURS

Every hostess wishes to vary the drinks she serves and I am sure she will find fruit juice sours a nice innovation.

JACK FROST SOUR

1 teaspoonful of powdered sugar,
1 egg,
½ cupful of sweet cream,

¼ cupful of apple juice (commercial),
½ cupful of cracked ice.

Pour the cream, sugar, commercial apple juice and ice into a shaker and shake thoroughly; strain into a tall, thin, stemmed glass and fill up with carbonated water, using a syphon.

SOUR À LA CREOLÉ

1 lime,
1 teaspoonful of powdered sugar,
1 tablespoonful of carbonated water,
¾ cupful of white grape juice,
6 drops of Jamaica ginger,
1 spoonful of ice cream,
   Fruit.

Put the juice of one lime in a shaker; mix the sugar and carbonated water thoroughly; add the grape juice and Jamaica ginger; strain into a tall glass and fill to within an inch of the top with carbonated water. Add a spoonful of ice cream, and any small fruit in season.

GRAPE JUICE SOUR

¼ cupful of purple grape juice,
1 teaspoonful of lime juice,
2 teaspoonfuls of powdered sugar,
2 teaspoonfuls of sweet cream,
½ cupful of shaved ice.

Pour the grape juice, lime juice, sugar, ice and cream in a shaker and shake thoroughly; strain and serve. A large claret glass may be used for this, or a tall, narrow, stemmed glass. If there should not be liquid enough to reach to within an inch of the top of the glass, add carbonated water.

SOUR DELICIOUS

1 lime,
1 teaspoonful of powdered sugar,
⅓ cupful of sparkling apple juice,
⅛ cupful of peach syrup (2 tablespoonfuls),
1 egg white,
  Ice.

Extract the juice from the lime, put it with the ice, sugar, syrup, egg white and apple juice in a shaker and shake well; strain into a serving glass and serve immediately.

FLORIDA SOUR

½ lemon,
½ orange,
¼ cupful of apricot syrup,
½ cupful of white grape juice,
  Ice.

Extract the juice from the half orange and the half lemon; pour it into the shaker with the ice, apricot syrup and the grape juice. Shake until thoroughly cold; strain into a tall, thin, long-stemmed glass and serve.

LOGANBERRY SOUR

¼ cupful of loganberry juice,
2 teaspoonfuls of sugar,
½ lemon,
  Apollinaris,
  Cherries,
  Ice.

Put the loganberry juice, sugar, the juice from half a lemon and a half cupful of cracked ice in a shaker; shake well, strain into a claret glass, fill up with Apollinaris and add several fresh cherries.

JERSEY SOUR

1 teaspoonful of powdered sugar,
1 teaspoonful of lemon juice,
½ cupful of apple juice,
   Ice.

Put the lemon juice, apple juice (commercial), sugar and ice in a shaker; shake well, strain into a claret glass and add two Maraschino cherries and serve.

RICKEYS FROM FRUIT JUICES

When one wearies of other mixed drinks, try a rickey made of fruit juice, and I am sure the experiment will be tried again.

GINGER RICKEY

1 lime,
½ cupful of ginger ale,
   Vichy,
   Ice.

Use a small, straight-sided tumbler, squeeze the lime juice into it, add two or three pieces of ice and the ginger ale; fill the glass with vichy.

WHITE GRAPE RICKEY

½ lime,
¾ cupful of white grape juice,
   Vichy,
   Ice.

Extract the juice from a half lime, pour into a medium fizz glass, add two tablespoonfuls of cracked ice, pour in the grape juice and fill the glass with vichy.

APPLE JUICE RICKEY

1 lime,
¾ cupful of commercial apple juice (sparkling),
Carbonated water,
Ice.

Extract the juice from the lime, put in a medium sized fizz glass, which is a straight-sided tumbler; add the apple juice and ice; fill the glass with carbonated water. Use a syphon.

ROYAL RICKEY

½ lime,
1 teaspoonful of powdered sugar,
¼ cupful of loganberry juice,
½ cupful of white grape juice,
Ice,
Vichy.

Pour the loganberry juice, lime juice, sugar and grape juice over the ice in a fizz glass; fill the glass nearly to the top with vichy. Serve.

COBBLERS

So many pleasant and refreshing drinks may be made of fruit juices, and I am quite sure that none are more satisfying than fruit juice cobblers. In drinks, as in anything the hostess sets before her guests, it is well to remember that if the eye be pleased the palate is more readily pleased. Cobblers are good to look at as well as refreshing to drink.

CATAWBA GRAPE COBBLER

1 teaspoonful of powdered sugar,
2 tablespoonfuls of carbonated water,
½ cupful of Catawba grape juice,
1 tablespoonful of orange juice,
Fruits, ice cream,
Ice.

Use a tall, stemmed glass; a dinner goblet is an excellent type. Put the sugar in the glass and add the carbonated water; enough to dissolve the sugar; add the grape juice; fill the glass with shaved ice, add the orange juice, decorate with any attractive fruits in season, such as strawberries, or cherries, pineapple and orange when strawberries cannot be obtained, and top with a spoonful of vanilla ice cream. Serve with a straw and a long handled spoon.

CONCORD GRAPE COBBLER

  1 teaspoonful of powdered sugar,
  2 tablespoonfuls of carbonated water,
  ½ cupful of Concord grape juice,
  ½ inch of preserved ginger,
  Ice,
  Fruits in season,
  Ice cream.

Put the sugar and carbonated water in a tall, thin, long-stemmed glass and stir: add the grape juice and fill the glass with shaved ice. Decorate with shredded pineapple and the ginger chopped fine. Top with a spoonful of ice cream. Serve with a straw and a long handled spoon.

MOCK CHAMPAGNE COBBLER

  ½ cupful of sparkling cider or apple juice,
  Strawberry ice cream,
  Ice,
  Candied cherries.

Use a champagne glass, and fill it with shaved ice. Pour in all the apple juice or sparkling cider the glass will hold; add four candied cherries and top with a spoonful of strawberry ice cream.

WHITE GRAPE JUICE COBBLER

1½ teaspoonfuls of powdered sugar,
⅜ cupful of carbonated water,
½ cupful of white grape juice,
⅜ cupful of shaved ice.

Make this cobbler in a tall goblet, placing the sugar in the glass first, then the carbonated water, dissolve, using a long handled spoon. Add the grape juice, and fill the glass with shaved ice. Decorate with skinned and seeded Malaga grapes, small pieces of pineapple, oranges or strawberries. In fact use such fruits as are in season. Serve with a straw and a spoon.

FLIPS FROM FRUITS

Even the name sounds cooling and frivolous and just the thing to try in warm weather.

CRÉOLE FLIP

1 teaspoonful of sugar,
½ cupful of white grape juice,
1 egg,
1 inch of preserved ginger,
   Nutmeg,
   Ice.

Put the sugar and grape juice in a shaker, stir until the sugar is dissolved; add one-third cupful of cracked ice, an inch of preserved ginger, chopped fine, and one egg. Shake this thoroughly, strain into a small, stemmed glass, sprinkle with grated nutmeg and serve.

VANILLA FLIP

1 teaspoonful of sugar,
1 cupful of top milk,
1 egg,
⅜ cupful of cracked ice,

Teaspoonful of vanilla extract,
Nutmeg.

Pour the milk, sugar, ice and egg into a shaker; shake well, strain into a thin, long stemmed glass, sprinkle the top with grated nutmeg and serve.

CHOCOLATE FLIP

1 teaspoonful of sugar,
2 tablespoonfuls of chocolate syrup,
1 cupful of top milk,
1 egg,
½ cupful of cracked ice,
½ teaspoonful of vanilla.

Pour all the ingredients into a cocktail shaker, and shake until thoroughly mixed and very cold. Strain into a tall, stemmed glass and serve.

RASPBERRY FLIP

1 teaspoonful of sugar,
3 tablespoonfuls of raspberry syrup,
1 egg,
½ cupful of white grape juice,
Carbonated water,
Ice.

Dissolve the sugar with a little carbonated water, add the raspberry syrup, the grape juice, ice and the egg; placing all in a shaker, shake well; strain into a long stemmed glass and fill with carbonated water.

JULEPS WHICH CHEER BUT DO NOT INEBRIATE

Try these delightful juleps and let me prove that I am right.

GINGER ALE JULEP

For each service, use:
2 sprays of mint,
½ lemon,
1 teaspoonful of sugar,
½ pint of ginger ale,
  Lemon peeling,
  Water,
  Ice.

If there are to be a number served, the lemon juice, lemon peel, sugar and a little water may be mixed, crushed with the mint, and allowed to stand on ice for half an hour before mixing. If one is to make only one or two drinks, it is as well to mix in the glasses.

Put one spray of mint in the glass, crush with a spoon; add the sugar, a piece of the lemon peel and a little water. Continue to mash with the spoon until the juice is extracted from the mint and some of the volatile oils are extracted from the lemon peeling, then remove the crushed mint and peeling. Add the lemon juice, stir and fill the glass, which should be a tall goblet, with crushed ice, then pour in the ginger ale. Place a fresh spray of mint in the glass and top with two or three Maraschino cherries. Serve with a straw.

GEORGIA MINT JULEP

1 teaspoonful of lemon juice,
1 teaspoonful of powdered sugar,
¼ cupful of peach syrup,
¾ cupful of white grape juice,
4 sprays of fresh mint,
  Ice.

Use a tall goblet; crush a spray of mint in the bottom of the glass, add the sugar and a very little water, and stir until the sugar dissolves; then add the peach syrup. Fill the glass nearly full with crushed ice and fill with grape juice. Add several fresh sprays of mint and serve.

TEA JULEP

This is made best in a quantity large enough to serve several people. The amount may be doubled or cut in two if the hostess wishes, however.

1 quart of tea infusion,
12 sprays of fresh mint,
2 oranges,
2 lemons,
½ a medium cucumber,
1 pint of ginger ale,
   Ice,
   Sugar.

Make the tea infusion by pouring a quart of water over two teaspoonfuls of tea and allowing it to stand for six minutes. When cool pour into a large bowl; add six sprays of mint, the oranges sliced thinly, the juice of the lemons, the half cucumber, peeled and sliced, and sugar to taste. This should stand on ice for an hour. When ready to serve remove the cucumber and the mint; pour into a tall glass pitcher which has been half filled with crushed ice. Add the remaining six sprays of mint and a dozen strawberries if in season, and last, add the ginger ale and serve.

APPLE JUICE JULEP

1 tablespoonful of powdered sugar,
2½ tablespoonfuls of water,
½ cupful of commercial apple juice,
4 sprays of mint,
1 teaspoonful of lemon juice,
   Ice.

Put the sugar, lemon juice and water into a tall goblet and stir until the sugar is dissolved; add two sprays of fresh mint and crush until the flavor of the mint is extracted; remove the mint, fill the glass nearly full of crushed ice and fill in with the apple juice; thrust the remaining sprays of mint into the ice and serve.

IV — FRUIT VINEGARS, SHRUBS AND WATERS

A generation or two ago every housewife who prided herself upon her ability as a hostess was very sure to have in her cellar shrubs and fruit vinegars of many kinds. For in this way she could always offer a guest a delightful and refreshing drink with the least amount of work and expenditure of time.

I have been fortunate to have found in the family recipes for vinegars and shrubs dating back to 1845. Besides these I shall give those of later dates, allowing my readers to try them and decide for themselves which they shall use.

RASPBERRY VINEGAR (date 1845)

2 quarts of raspberries,
1 pint of cider vinegar,
  Sugar.

To two quarts of raspberries use one pint of cider vinegar. Allow this to stand for two or three days; then mash and put them in a bag to strain. To every pint of juice, when strained, add a pound of granulated sugar. Boil this for twenty minutes, skim and bottle when cold.

RASPBERRY VINEGAR (MOTHER'S)

10 quarts of red raspberries,
  Cider vinegar,
  Sugar.

Look over ten quarts of red raspberries and cover with cider vinegar. Allow this to stand for two or three days, then strain and press the juice from the berries. To every pint of juice add one pound of sugar, and boil until of the consistency of syrup. Bottle and store for use. A table-spoonful to a glass of iced water is an excellent proportion.

RASPBERRY VINEGAR (CRÉOLE RECIPE)

2 quarts of raspberries,
1 quart of French vinegar,
  Sugar.

Put one quart of the berries in a deep crock and pour the vinegar over them, allowing this to stand for twenty-four hours. Strain through a jelly bag, add the other quart of berries and allow them to stand another twenty-four hours. Strain again, adding the berries, allow this to stand for a third time for twenty-four hours. Then strain through a muslin bag and add one pound of granulated sugar for each pint of juice. Boil the whole for half an hour, using a porcelain kettle. When cold, bottle and seal. Kept in a cool place this will keep for years, improving with age.

Créoles use this vinegar by adding a teaspoonful to a small glass of iced water, sometimes putting a little more sugar with it, as pleases the taste of the guest.

BLACKBERRY VINEGAR (NEW ENGLAND RECIPE

10 quarts of blackberries,
   Cider vinegar,
   Sugar.

Cover ten quarts of blackberries with cider vinegar and allow to stand for three days, strain and press all the juice possible from the berries, using a jelly bag. To every pint of juice add one pound of granulated sugar and boil for twenty minutes. Skim, and when cold bottle and seal.

To serve, use a tablespoonful to a glass of iced water.

BLACKBERRY VINEGAR (CRÉOLE RECIPE)

2 quarts of blackberries,
1 quart of French vinegar,
  Sugar.

Put one quart of blackberries into a deep jar and pour the vinegar over. Allow this to stand for twenty-four hours, strain, add the other quart of berries, returning the first berries, allow this to again stand for twenty-four hours. Strain again, returning the berries, allow it to stand for the third twenty-four hours. Strain through a muslin bag, and add a pound of sugar for every pint of juice. Boil in a porcelain kettle for a half hour. When cold, bottle and keep in a cool place. This vinegar will improve with age. Use a teaspoonful to a *small* glass of iced water, when serving.

STRAWBERRY VINEGAR

10 quarts of strawberries,
  Vinegar,
  Sugar.

Hull the berries and cover them with a pure cider vinegar, allowing them to stand twenty-four hours. Strain, and press all the juice possible from the berries, using a jelly bag for the straining. Add one pound of granulated sugar to each pint of juice and boil for twenty minutes. When cold, bottle and seal and keep in a cool place. Use one tablespoonful to the glass when ready to serve.

STRAWBERRY VINEGAR (CRÉOLE RECIPE)

2 quarts of strawberries,
1 quart of French vinegar,
  Sugar.

Pour a quart of vinegar over one quart of berries, using a deep dish; allow this to stand for twenty-four hours, strain, add the second quart of berries and again allow to stand for twenty-four hours, repeat the same operation the next day, making three times in all, then strain through a muslin bag, and add one pound of sugar for each pint of juice. Boil the mixture for a half hour using a porcelain kettle. When cold, bottle and seal. Use one tablespoonful to each small glass of iced water, when serving.

PINEAPPLE VINEGAR

3 ripe pineapples,
1 quart of pure cider vinegar,
  Sugar.

Peel and slice the pineapples very thin and cover with pure cider vinegar, allowing it to stand three days. Mash well, and strain through a bag. To every quart of juice allow one and three-quarters pounds of granulated sugar. Boil for ten minutes, skim carefully and bottle when slightly cool. Use a tablespoonful to each glass of iced water when serving.

ORANGE VINEGAR

3 dozen oranges,
1 quart of cider vinegar,
  Sugar.

Peel the oranges carefully, slice very thin and cover with the vinegar, allowing them to stand for three days. Mash well, and strain through a jelly bag. To each quart of juice allow one and three-quarters pounds of granulated sugar. Boil for ten minutes, allow to cool slightly; bottle and seal. Keep in a cool place. One tablespoonful of this added to a glass of iced water makes a delicious drink.

CURRANT SHRUB (date of recipe, 1845)

2 quarts of currants,
  Sugar.

Crush the currants and press through a bag; to each pint of juice add a pound of granulated sugar, boil five minutes, stir constantly while cooling. When cool, bottle and seal. Use a teaspoonful of this syrup to a glass of iced water.

RASPBERRY SHRUB

Put the raspberries in a porcelain utensil and crush with a wooden spoon. Cover with cider vinegar and let stand over night. Strain the juice through a jelly bag, add three-fourths of a pound of sugar for every pint of the juice. Heat slowly to the boiling point, skim, allow to boil five minutes and then bottle while hot. Seal the corks with paraffin or sealing wax.

FRUIT WATERS

Fruit waters are prepared shortly before they are to be used, are not bottled and stored as are syrups. So it is necessary to make these waters only when the fruit to be used is in season.

CHERRY WATER

2 pounds of cherries,
1 lemon,
½ pound of sugar.

Stone the cherries, mash the pulp well, using a porcelain vessel; add a cupful of distilled water (or rain water if it is possible to obtain it fresh and clear), and the juice of one lemon. Stir well and allow to stand for two hours. Wash the cherry stones, crush and add to the cherry pulp; add half a pound of granulated sugar and allow to stand for another hour. Strain this mixture and filter, using a jelly bag. Put into a jar and set on the ice until ready for use. Fill glasses nearly full of crushed ice and fill with the fruit water.

ORANGE WATER

6 oranges (preferably Florida oranges),
1 ounce of orange flower water (commercial),
1 lemon,
1 cupful of sugar,
1 pint of distilled water.

Extract the juice from the oranges and the lemon; put in an earthen dish, add the orange flower water, distilled water, and the sugar. Stir until the sugar is dissolved, strain carefully and put on ice until ready to serve. Fill the glass nearly full with crushed ice and fill with the orange water.

STRAWBERRY WATER

1 quart of water,
½ pound of sugar,
  Ripe strawberries.

Select ripe strawberries, crush and strain, pressing all the juice possible from them. To each pint of juice, add one quart of distilled water and a half pound of granulated sugar. Stir until the sugar is dissolved and place on ice until ready to serve. Fill the serving glass nearly full of crushed ice and fill with the strawberry water.

RASPBERRY WATER

Raspberries to make ½ pint of juice,
½ pound of sugar,
1 quart of water.

Select ripe berries; look them over carefully, as little worms get into raspberries. Crush the berries, add a little distilled water, allowing them to stand for an hour. Strain through a jelly bag, squeezing all the juice possible from them. To a pint of juice add a half pound of granulated sugar and the remaining distilled water. Stir well and place on ice until ready to use. A teaspoonful to a small glass of crushed ice makes a desirable drink for hot days.

CURRANT WATER

½ pound of sugar,
1 quart of water,
   Currants to make ½ pint of juice.

Mash the currants, add a little of the quart of distilled water, and put on the ice for an hour. At the end of that time, strain through a jelly bag; add the sugar and the rest of the distilled water. Stir, and set on the ice until time for service. A generous teaspoonful to a small glass of crushed ice, or a tablespoonful to a glass of iced water is about the amount which will prove pleasing to one's guests.

PINEAPPLE WATER

1 large ripe pineapple,
½ pound of sugar,
1 lemon,
1 quart of distilled water.

Peel the pineapple carefully, cut into thin slices, mash and allow to stand for ten minutes. Press as much of the juice as possible through a sieve, then allow it to drip through a jelly bag. Add the sugar and the water, stir and set on the ice until ready to serve. Into a claret glass of crushed ice put two teaspoonfuls of the juice, or into a small glass of iced water, put two tablespoonfuls of the juice.

V — SYRUPS — FRUIT AND PLAIN

As many delightful drinks are made with either plain or fruit syrup as the foundation, I shall give a number of recipes for making these, leaving the housekeeper to decide which she prefers.

PLAIN SYRUP

The following recipe is one used by a man famous for his ability in mixing drinks:

6½ pounds of loaf sugar,
½ gallon of water,
1 egg white.

Boil the sugar, water and egg white together until the sugar is thoroughly dissolved; filter through flannel, bottle and seal.

Note: When using a flannel bag, wring it out of very hot water before using, being sure that it is as dry as you can make it. In this way there will be very little loss of syrup.

PLAIN SYRUP No. 2

1½ quarts of water,
2 pounds of loaf sugar.

This recipe is also one used by a well-known mixer of drinks.

Put the sugar and water over the fire in an enameled kettle; allow it to boil slowly; stirring occasionally. Skim well, and strain into bottles and seal.

PLAIN SYRUP (CRÉOLE RECIPE)

2 pounds of sugar,
1½ pints of water.

Cook the sugar and water until the syrup snaps instantly if placed between the fingers and the fingers are immersed in cold water. Allow this to become somewhat cool, bottle and seal.

PLAIN SYRUP (OLD RECIPE)

The recipe reads: " To every large teacupful of water, add a pound of sugar." It would seem wiser in this day to use one *measuring* cupful of water to each pound of granulated sugar, if one cares to use this recipe. For what one might consider a large cup someone else might think rather small.

The recipe directs that "as the sugar and water begins to heat, stir it often, and when it rises towards the top of the kettle, put in another cupful of water; repeating this process two or three times." If the syrup is not clear, and a scum arises, we are told " to skim it carefully, and strain into bottles."

PLAIN SYRUP (QUICKLY MADE)

4 pounds of granulated sugar,
1 quart of cold water,
1 egg white.

Put the sugar in a porcelain kettle, add the stiffly beaten white of one egg, and the quart of water; stir until the sugar is thoroughly dissolved. Put over the fire and simmer for five minutes, skim, strain through a flannel bag, bottle and seal. It is always well to make a small quantity, for in that way one is assured that there will be no spoilage.

When using a flannel bag, be sure to wring it very dry from hot water, by so doing insuring the least loss of syrup.

GUM SYRUP

Sometimes one reads a recipe in which " gum " is used, and unless one is initiated one is not apt to know what is required.

3½ pounds of loaf sugar,
2 quarts of water.

Boil together for five minutes, strain and bottle.

APRICOT SYRUP (CRÉOLE RECIPE)

3 pints of apricot juice,
1 quart of plain syrup (use Créole recipe for plain syrup),
1 teaspoonful of extract of apricot.

Peel and stone the apricots, cut into small pieces, mash well, cover with a linen cloth, and set them on the ice in a stone or porcelain jar for thirty-six hours. Then strain through a bag, pressing out all the juice possible. Heat the plain syrup until the boiling point is reached, add the apricot juice and boil hard for five minutes. Take from the fire and allow to become nearly cold; add the extract, bottle and keep in a cool place.

APRICOT SYRUP

1 pint of apricot juice.
1 pound of sugar.

Peel and cut into pieces as many apricots as one wishes to use, put into a porcelain kettle with a little water — enough to barely cover the bottom of the kettle; crack a few of the apricot stones and add to the fruit and water. Boil slowly for fifteen minutes, strain through a flannel bag. To each pint of juice use one pound of sugar, return to the kettle and boil for five minutes. Pour into hot bottles and seal.

BLACKBERRY SYRUP (CRÉOLE RECIPE)

3 pints of blackberry juice,
1 quart of plain syrup.

Look the blackberries over very carefully, wash, stem

and mash; cover carefully with a cloth and set on ice for thirty-six hours. Strain through a bag, pressing out all the juice possible. Heat the plain syrup to the boiling point and add the blackberry juice, boil for five minutes, remove from the fire and allow to become nearly cool; bottle and seal. Put in a cool place when storing.

BLACKBERRY SYRUP

1 pint of blackberry juice,
1 pound of granulated sugar,
1 ounce of cider vinegar,
4 whole cloves,
⅛ teaspoonful of cinnamon,
⅛ teaspoonful of ground mace.

Select perfectly ripe blackberries, wash, mash and put on the ice in a carefully covered jar for twenty-four hours. It is well to cover the berries with a linen cloth. At the end of that time, press through a bag, and to each pint of juice add one pound of granulated sugar, one ounce of cider vinegar, four whole cloves, an eighth teaspoonful of cinnamon and an eighth teaspoonful of mace. Bring to the boiling point and allow it to boil for five minutes, strain into hot bottles and seal. When cold, store in a cool place.

CHERRY SYRUP

1 pint of cherry juice,
1 pound of granulated sugar.

Mash enough washed and stemmed cherries to make a pint of juice; let the mashed cherries stand on ice for twenty-four hours. Strain through a bag, add one pound of sugar to each pint of juice, boil five minutes, skim, if necessary and pour into hot bottles; seal and store in a cool place.

CHERRY SYRUP (CRÉOLE RECIPE)

3 pints of cherry juice,
1 quart of plain syrup.

Wash, stem and pit the cherries; mash them and place on ice for thirty-six hours. Press the juice through a bag, measure, and to each 3 pints of juice use one quart of plain syrup. Heat the syrup to the boiling point, add the fruit juice and boil for five minutes. Allow to become nearly cold, bottle and seal. Store in a cool place.

CHERRY SYRUP (NEW ENGLAND RECIPE)

1 pint of cherry juice,
1 pound of sugar.

Wash, stem and mash enough cherries to make a pint of juice, using a porcelain vessel; crush a few pits and add to the cherries; allow the fruit to stand on ice for twenty-four hours. Strain, and press all the juice possible through a bag. To each pint of juice, add one pound of granulated sugar, bring to the boiling point and boil for five minutes. Skim, if necessary, and put into hot bottles. Seal and store.

CURRANT SYRUP

1 pint of currant juice,
1 pound of sugar.

Stem, wash and mash enough currants to make a pint of juice. Cover and stand on ice for twenty-four hours. Strain through a bag, squeezing out all the juice possible. To each pint add one pound of granulated sugar, and boil for five minutes. Skim, if necessary, bottle in hot bottles, seal and store in a cool place.

GRAPE SYRUP (CRÉOLE RECIPE)

1 quart of plain syrup,
1 pint of grape juice (made at home),
1 pint of Catawba grape juice (commercial).

Wash, stem and seed the grapes; crush and set on ice for

thirty-six hours. Strain through a bag, add the Catawba juice, and add that to the plain syrup, which should have been brought to the boiling point. Mix and boil together for five minutes. Strain, and when nearly cold, bottle and store.

LEMON SYRUP

4 pounds of sugar,
1 quart of water,
2 cupfuls of lemon juice.

Boil the water and sugar together for ten minutes, add the lemon juice, continue boiling for another five minutes, strain into hot bottles and store.

ORANGE SYRUP

1 pint of orange juice,
½ cupful of lemon juice,
1 quart of plain syrup (see recipe).

Bring the plain syrup to the boiling point, add the lemon and orange juice, continue to boil for five minutes. Strain into hot bottles and store in a cool place.

ORGEAT SYRUP (CRÉOLE RECIPE)

A very little of this syrup used in drinks where a mixture of fruits is used will be found most satisfactory.

1 pound of sweet almonds,
4 ounces of bitter almonds,
2 pounds of granulated sugar,
1 quart of soft water (distilled, if preferred),
1 lemon,
2 ounces of orange flower water.

Shell the almonds, and throw into *cold* water, allowing them to stand until the skin will come off readily. Mash them, using a mortar, if possible, or an earthen dish; continue to crush and mash, adding a few drops of water and a little of the zest of the lemon, until the mixture is paste-like. Moisten this paste with half of the soft water, and squeeze as much as possible through a firm bag. Return the paste to the dish and add the rest of the water, stir, put into the bag again and again press all through the bag that is possible.

Bring the plain syrup to the boiling point; remove from the fire, stir the almond milk in thoroughly, return to the fire and bring again to the boiling point, allowing it to boil for five minutes. When cool, add the orange flower water; stir well, being sure that it is well blended. Strain again, and place in bottles; seal and store. It is well, however, to watch this and shake the bottles once in a while, especially if the almond oil has risen to the top.

ORANGE FLOWER SYRUP

1 pint of orange flower water,
1½ pounds of granulated sugar.

Put the sugar into a porcelain kettle with the orange flower water, stir until the sugar is dissolved, place on the fire and slowly bring to the boiling point. Remove from the fire, cool somewhat and bottle. Store in a cool place.

PEACH SYRUP

1 pint of peach juice,
1 pound of sugar,
½ teaspoonful of peach extract.

Peel the peaches by dropping them into boiling water for one minute, then the skin may be rubbed off, wasting none of the fruit at all. Cut the peaches in small pieces, crack a few peach stones and add to the fruit, placing all in a porcelain kettle; cover the bottom of the kettle with water and boil slowly for fifteen minutes, strain through a flannel bag, add one pound of sugar to each pint of juice and bring to the boiling point again, boil for five minutes; take from the fire, add the peach extract and bottle in hot bottles.

PINEAPPLE SYRUP

1 pint of pineapple juice,
1 quart of plain syrup,
½ cupful of lemon juice.

Peel the pineapple, remove the eyes, using a pineapple scissors if possible, for in that manner it is possible to remove *all* the eye with the least amount of trouble. Wind a towel around the pines, and grate the pineapple on a coarse grater. Be sure to hold the pineapple over a porcelain kettle or dish while working with it, so saving all the juice. Heat a quart of plain syrup until it begins to boil, add the pint of pineapple juice, and boil for five minutes; take from the fire and add the lemon juice. Bottle while hot, using hot bottles. Seal and store in a cool place.

RASPBERRY SYRUP

1 pint of raspberry juice,
1 pound of sugar.

Pick all the stems from the berries and look them over very carefully as there are many little insects which like to hide in raspberries. Wash and mash thoroughly. Place on ice for twenty-four hours, strain through a bag and add one pound of sugar to each pint of juice. Bring this to the boiling point and boil for five minutes. Strain into hot bottles and seal. Keep in a cool place, preferably a dark one.

RASPBERRY AND CURRANT SYRUP

½ pint of raspberry juice,
½ pint of currant juice,
1 pound of sugar.

Remove the stems, and discard any imperfect berries, remove the stems and wash the currants; place in a bowl or porcelain kettle and mash thoroughly. Place on ice, closely covered with a fine cloth, for twenty-four hours. Strain through a bag and add one pound of granulated sugar to each pint of juice. Boil for five minutes and put in hot bottles. Seal the bottles and place in a cool dark place until ready to use.

STRAWBERRY SYRUP

1 pint of strawberry juice,
1 pound of sugar.

Select ripe berries only, but be sure that they are not over-ripe. Hull them, put them in a bowl or porcelain kettle, mash well, cover with a cloth and place on ice for ten hours. Strain through a bag, pressing out all the juice possible. To each pint of juice add one pound of granulated sugar, put over a slow fire, stir constantly, and when the boiling point is reached, skim and bottle while hot. Use hot bottles, seal and store in a cool dark place.

LIME SYRUP

1 pint of lime juice (use fresh limes),
1 quart of plain syrup.

Extract the juice from the limes; bring the plain syrup to the boiling point, add the lime juice, continue to boil for five minutes longer. Strain into hot bottles and seal. Store where it is both dark and cool.

CHOCOLATE SYRUPS

If one would be able to serve cold chocolate drinks at home which will rival those offered at the soda fountains, one must learn how to make chocolate syrups and keep them bottled for an emergency.

CHOCOLATE SYRUP (FOR BOTTLING)

1½ pounds of cocoa,
1½ pints of water,
1½ pounds of sugar,
 1 teaspoonful of vanilla.

Heat the water until boiling, and use a little of it to
moisten the cocoa, mixing it until smooth; add the sugar,
and the rest of the water, stir carefully, being sure that
the mixture is smooth, put over the fire and bring to the
boiling point; boil for five minutes and pour into sterilized
bottles.   Seal and put away in a cool place.

CHOCOLATE SYRUP (FOR IMMEDIATE USE)

½ cupful of cocoa,
2 cupfuls of sugar,
1 cupful of boiling water,
 Vanilla.

Mix the cocoa and sugar, stir in a little of the water,
mixing well to be sure that the mixture is smooth; then add
the rest of the water, stir well and boil for five minutes.
Add a half teaspoonful of vanilla and put into a pint jar
until needed for the refreshing drink.

Two tablespoonfuls to each glass is about the right proportion when ready to serve.

CHOCOLATE SYRUP (MADE FROM UN-
SWEETENED CHOCOLATE)

Because chocolate is somewhat richer than cocoa, many
prefer it.   The following recipe, easily made, will be found
most satisfactory.

½ pound of grated chocolate,
1 cupful of granulated sugar,
1 cupful of water,
½ teaspoonful of vanilla.

Grate the chocolate, add the sugar and then the hot water, mixing well. Bring to the boiling point, boil for ten minutes, and put in a cool place until serving time. A fruit jar is a most acceptable receptacle.

COFFEE SYRUP

¼ pound of Java coffee,
¼ pound of Mocha coffee,
¼ gallon of water,
5 pounds of granulated sugar.

Grind the coffee, add the cold water and boil for five minutes; strain and add the sugar; boil up again, strain a second time and bottle while hot.

COFFEE SYRUP No. 2

½ cupful of powdered coffee,
3 cupfuls of boiling water,
3 tablespoonfuls of granulated sugar.

Use any coffee desired, although a mixture of Java and Mocha is recommended. Pulverize the coffee, pack it in the bag of a drip pot; pour the boiling water over it slowly, allow it to drip until the powdered coffee in the bag seems dry. Add the sugar, boil for five minutes and bottle while hot. Use hot bottles, and seal immediately.

CREAM SYRUP

½ pint of thick cream,
½ pint of milk,
1 pound of block sugar.

Pour enough hot water over the sugar to melt it, add the milk, stir until the sugar is dissolved and add the cream; mix well and it is ready for use.

SARSAPARILLA SYRUP

10 drops of oil of wintergreen,
10 drops of oil of sassafras,
¼ ounce of fluid extract of liquorice,
5 pints of plain syrup.

Heat the plain syrup until the boiling point is reached, and stir in the essential oils. Bottle while hot.

VI — GRAPE JUICE, ROOT BEERS AND CIDER

GRAPE JUICE

As it is possible to purchase grape juice, either purple or white, in bottles, at prices which are not at all beyond reason, it is hardly necessary to make it at home, but if one has a few grapes which one desires to use for drinks and has not the opportunity to obtain the commercial product it may be made after the directions issued by the Department of Agriculture at Washington.

These directions follow.

TO MAKE GRAPE JUICE

Only clean, sound, well ripened, but not overripe, grapes should be used. These may be crushed and pressed either by hand or in an ordinary cider mill. If light colored juice is desired, the crushed grapes are put in a clean, well washed cloth sack and either hung up and twisted or grasped by two persons, one at either end, and twisted until the greater part of the juice is expressed. Then, in a double boiler or its equivalent, such as a large stone jar placed in a pan of hot water, so that the juice does not come in direct contact with the fire, the juice is gradually heated to a temperature of 180° to 200° F. The temperature should never be allowed to go over 200° F. It is best to use a thermometer; if none is available, however, the juice may be heated until it steams, but it should not be allowed to boil. It should be poured immediately into a glass or enameled vessel and allowed to settle for 24 hours; then the juice should be drained from the sediment and run through several thicknesses of clean flannel or through a conic filter made from woolen cloth or felt and fixed to a hoop of iron, so that it can be suspended wherever necessary. The juice is then poured into clean bottles, space being left at the top for the liquid to expand when heated. A good home substitute for the commercial pasteurizer is an ordinary wash boiler with a thin board fitted over the bottom on which the filled bottles are set. Ordinary glass fruit jars serve the same purpose equally well. The tubs should be filled with water within an inch or so of the tops of the bottles and heated until the water begins to simmer. The bottles should be taken out and sealed or corked immediately. Only new corks that have just been soaked in a temperature of about 140° F. should be used. It is well to take the further precaution of sealing the corks with paraffin or sealing wax to prevent the entrance of mold germs.

When red juice is desired, crushed grapes should first be heated to a temperature of not more than 200° F.; then strained through a clean cloth or drip bag, no pressure being used, and set away to cool and settle. The remaining procedure is the same for the red as for the light-colored juice. Many people do not even take the trouble to let the juice settle after it is strained, simply reheating and sealing the vessels and setting them away in an upright position in a cool place where they will be undisturbed. If bottles are used, the corks should be sterilized and the necks of the bottles sealed with sealing wax. The juice settles, and when desired for use the clear liquid is poured off the sediment.

Any person familiar with the process of canning fruit can put up grape juice, for the principles involved are the same. Care should be taken not to sterilize the juice at a temperature higher than 195° F.; or the finished product will have a scorched taste. The bottles or jars should not be so large that when they are opened the juice will spoil before it can be used. Unfermented grape juice, properly made and bottled, will keep indefinitely if not exposed to the atmosphere or to infection of mold germs; when a bottle is once open, however, the contents, like canned goods generally, should be used as soon as possible. Unfermented juice may be made not only from all varieties of grapes, but also from some other fruits, such as apples, pears and cherries.　Some berries also yield excellent juices.

GRAPE JUICE No. 2

Crush the grapes in a clean kettle with a wooden spoon and put them in a cloth sack or jelly bag.　Twist the sack or press it until the juice has all come out.　Put the juice in a double boiler over hot water until it steams.　If a kettle is used, great care must be taken that the juice does not boil.　Let the juice stand in an enamel kettle for 24 hours to settle.　Run it through a flannel jelly bag and put into clean bottles.　Leave space in bottle for the liquid to expand.　Put the bottle in a sterilizer and fill the sterilizer with cold water until within an inch of the top of the bottles. Heat the water slowly until it is nearly simmering, take the bottles out and insert clean corks, and, as a final precaution it is advisable to dip the top of the cork in sealing wax or paraffin.

This makes a light colored juice.　For a red juice, the grapes may be heated until just before the boiling point as in the first part of the process.　It is not necessary to allow the juice to settle but it is much clearer if you do.

GINGER BEER

2 ounces of ginger root,
2 ounces of cream of tartar,
1 lemon,
1½ pounds of granulated sugar,
¼ cake of compressed yeast.

Place the ginger in a large bowl, bruise and pound thoroughly; add boiling water, then the grated rind of the lemon and when stirred in, add the juice of the lemon.　Now mix in the cream of tartar and the sugar; stir well, allow to cool until lukewarm; add the yeast which should have been dissolved in a little warm water. Mix all together, cover tightly and allow to stand for six hours. At the end of that time, strain and put into bottles having patent tops, unless one has a commercial " topper " which is most desirable. Keep in a cool place, for if kept warm or not securely corked the beer will effervesce.

ENGLISH GINGER BEER

This interesting recipe dates back to about 1840.

1½ ounces of ginger,
4 quarts of boiling water,
1 ounce of cream of tartar,
1 pound of sugar,
2 lemons,
1 cupful of yeast.

Pour the boiling water upon the ginger and the sugar (either brown or granulated may be used) add two lemons thinly sliced. Into this pour one cupful of good yeast and allow it to stand for twenty-four hours. Pour off carefully and put into bottles.

MAPLE BEER

4 gallons of boiling water,
1 quart of pure maple syrup,
1 tablespoonful of essence of spruce,
1 pint of yeast.

This recipe too, dates back to 1840.

Put in a large container, one quart of pure maple syrup, and add one gallon of boiling water and the spruce essence; allow this to stand until lukewarm, then add a pint of yeast, allowing it to stand twenty-four hours. Pour off carefully and bottle and seal.

ROOT BEER

¼ cupful of commercial root beer extract,
5 pounds of sugar,
5 gallons of rain water,
¼ cake of compressed yeast.

Dissolve the yeast cake in a little warm water; mix the sugar and root beer extract together and add the water, which should be hot; allow this to stand until lukewarm and add the yeast cake; mix well, allow to settle and pour into bottles. If one owns patent top bottles they are easily handled. Fasten the stopper and store where it is cool. The beer will be ready for use after twenty-four hours.

It is not at all necessary to put this beer up in such quantities; just divide or subdivide the recipe.

SPRUCE BEER (CRÉOLE RECIPE)

2 quarts of water,
¼ ounce of hops,
½ teaspoonful of ginger,
¼ pint of Louisiana molasses,
4 tablespoonfuls of yeast,
  Sprigs of spruce.

Gather a handful of spruce sprigs, break and bruise, and steep in a little water until a strong essence is made.

Pour the water over the hops and the ginger and allow to boil; strain and add the molasses and essence of spruce. Cool until lukewarm and add the yeast. Cover tightly and stand away for twenty-four hours. Pour off carefully and bottle. Seal and store in a cool place. In two days the beer is ready for use.

One may gather the spruce sprigs as directed, or purchase the extract or essence of spruce, or steep the spruce gum.

BIRCH BEER

¼ pound of black birch bark,
½ ounce of hops,
1 teaspoonful of ginger,
½ compressed yeast cake,
1 pint of corn syrup,
3 quarts of water (soft or rain water).

Boil the birch bark in a quart of water until reduced a third; strain and set aside until the hops, syrup and ginger has boiled for twenty minutes. Strain and mix with the birch extract; when cooled until about lukewarm add the yeast cake dissolved in a little warm water. Cover tightly and stand away for twenty-four hours. Strain into bottles and cork well.

CIDER

It would seem unnecessary labor to make cider at home, unless, of course one lives on a farm and has many apples to dispose of after the selected apples are shipped or stored for winter use. And even in that event one is likely to take the apples to a community cider mill. But if there should be a time when one of my readers cares to try cider making at home it may be done with utensils found in every kitchen.

Be sure that there are no bruised or rotted spots on the apples to be used and wipe them carefully with a damp cloth. Cut them in pieces and run through a food grinder, placing a deep dish where it will catch *all* of the juice. Place a fine cloth in a colander; pile the apple pomace (the ground apple) in it and pour all the juice in too. Fold the cloth over and place a heavy weight on top, pressing it often. When the juice or cider is pressed out, bottle and use. It should not be kept, as it becomes sour very quickly.

It is probably as economical to purchase the sweet cider as to use the time and the necessary apples to make the cider.

TO KEEP CIDER SWEET AND SPARKLING

(Date of recipe, 1845)

Let the new sweet cider ferment from one to three weeks according to whether the weather is cool or warm, longer if cool or one week if warm. When it has attained a lively fermentation, add to each gallon, according to its acidity, from one-half to two pounds of sugar, and allow it to again ferment until the desired sweetness is reached. Pour out one quart of the cider and add for each gallon one-quarter ounce of sulphite of lime (anti-chloride). Stir the powder and cider until thoroughly mixed and return to the rest of the cider. Agitate well and briskly for a few minutes and then let the cider settle. The fermentation will cease at once. After a few days draw off the clear cider, bottle carefully, and cork well. Bottles with patent stoppers will be found most satisfactory.

TO BOIL CIDER

(Old New England recipe)

Use perfectly sweet cider, preferably not over two days old: boil until boiled down about half. Skim often, pour into hot bottles and cork tightly. Store in a cool place.

This may be used for drinks, by stirring two tablespoonfuls into a glassful of iced water.

VII — COLD MILK DRINKS, HOT MILK AND BUTTERMILK

SHAKES, NOGGS AND PUNCHES

While many do not care for milk as a drink, still milk in combination with syrups, eggs, malted milk, flavoring extracts or fruit juices will be found pleasing even to those who would not drink it plain. When one considers the amount of nourishment furnished by a glass of milk, it is well to serve it when possible, even disguised as a nogg or punch.

CHOCOLATE MILK

1 cupful of milk,
⅛ cupful of chocolate syrup (see syrups) (2 tablespoonfuls),
  Ice.

Use a cocktail shaker, put two tablespoonfuls of cracked ice in the shaker, add the chocolate syrup and the milk; shake well, strain into a tall glass and serve. It is wise to use an iced-tea glass, as these glasses hold at least ten ounces, and as a measuring cup will hold eight ounces of milk, there is room for the ice and syrup.

CHOCOLATE, EGG AND MILK

1 cupful of milk,
1 egg,
⅛ cupful of chocolate syrup (2 tablespoonfuls),
  Ice.

Place all the ingredients in a cocktail shaker, shake thoroughly and strain into a tall thin glass. There is enough nourishment in a drink of this sort to be used as a substitute for luncheon if one is too hurried to take time for a comfortable luncheon, slowly eaten.

COCOA NOGG

⅞ cupful of milk,
⅛ cupful of cocoa syrup (2 tablespoonfuls),
1 egg,
  Ice.

Separate the white and the yolk of the egg, whip the white until dry and stiff, put the yolk, ice, cocoa syrup and the milk into a shaker and shake well; pour about three-quarters of the mixture into a tall glass, pour the rest over the beaten white, stir it swiftly, and add to the mixture in the glass.

CHOCOLATE CREAM FLOAT

For each service use:
2 tablespoonfuls of chocolate syrup,
½ cupful of milk,
¼ cupful of thick cream,
  Powdered sugar,
  Vanilla.

Multiply this recipe by the number of persons to be served, making the full amount, serving in glasses as desired.

Select attractive glasses, narrow, tall, stemmed glasses are the best; fill them nearly to the top with finely cracked ice, put two tablespoonfuls of chocolate syrup into each glass, add a half cupful of milk; fill with stiffly whipped cream. When whipping the cream add enough powdered sugar to make it slightly sweet and stir in a few drops of vanilla.

CHOCOLATE SHAKE

1 cupful of milk,
2 tablespoonfuls of chocolate syrup,
1 egg,

Ice,
Vanilla.

Whip the white and the yolk of the egg separately. Put the yolk, ice, milk, chocolate and a few drops of vanilla in a cocktail shaker and shake well for at least two minutes. Put the stiffly whipped white in a tall glass, pour the chocolate mixture over, stirring it in slightly, and serve. Serve with a straw.

CHOCOLATE PUNCH

1 egg,
1 cupful of milk,
$\frac{1}{8}$ cupful of chocolate syrup (2 tablespoonfuls),
Nutmeg,
Few drops of vanilla,
Ice,
Ice cream.

Put the egg, milk, chocolate syrup, vanilla and ice in a cocktail shaker, shake for three minutes, strain into a tall thin glass and add a generous grating of nutmeg and top with a spoonful of vanilla ice cream.

CHOCOLATE CREAM PUNCH

1 egg,
1 cupful of milk,
$\frac{1}{8}$ cupful of chocolate syrup (2 tablespoonfuls),
$\frac{1}{8}$ cupful of thick cream,
Ice,
Sugar.

Whip the cream until stiff, adding a little powdered sugar, put the egg, milk, chocolate syrup and a little cracked ice in a shaker; shake well, strain into a tall thin glass and top with the whipped cream. Serve with a long handled spoon.

CHOCOLATE SODA

½ cupful of top milk,
⅛ cupful of chocolate syrup (2 tablespoonfuls),
2 tablespoonfuls of vanilla ice cream,
  Carbonated water.

Put the chocolate syrup in a tall glass, then the top milk, or milk and cream mixed, add two tablespoonfuls of ice cream; fill the glass with carbonated water, using a syphon. Serve with a long handled spoon.   One may use chocolate ice cream if one prefers.

COFFEE, EGG AND MILK

¾ cupful of dripped coffee,
2 tablespoonfuls of plain syrup,
1 egg,
¼ cupful of top milk,
  Ice.

Put the egg, ice, milk, coffee and syrup in a cocktail shaker and shake thoroughly for two minutes; strain into a tall thin glass and serve at once.

COFFEE PUNCH

¼ cupful of dripped coffee,
2 tablespoonfuls of plain syrup,
¼ cupful of top milk,
1 egg,
2 tablespoonfuls of vanilla ice cream,
¼ cupful of whipped cream, or marshmallow cream.

Put the dripped coffee, two pieces of ice, the egg, syrup and top milk in a shaker. Shake well, strain into a tall thin glass, add the ice cream, top with whipped cream or a tablespoonful of marshmallow cream. Serve with a long handled spoon.

COFFEE FOAM

1 cupful of milk,
1 egg,
⅓ cupful of dripped coffee,
2 tablespoonfuls of plain syrup.

Separate the yolk and the white of the egg; whip the white dry and stiff; put the yolk, milk and coffee in a shaker and shake well. Pour the mixture into a tall glass, reserving about a quarter; mix this with the egg white quickly and add to the top of the glass. Serve with a straw or long handled spoon.

COFFEE CREAM

½ cupful of milk,
½ cupful of thick cream,
⅓ cupful of dripped coffee,
1 egg,
1½ tablespoonfuls of plain syrup,
    Ice.

Put the ice, milk, coffee and the yolk of the egg in the shaker and shake well. Beat the egg white until dry and whip the cream until stiff. Pour the coffee and milk mixture over the egg white, stir swiftly, blending thoroughly; pour into a tall glass and add the whipped cream, which should be sweetened slightly. Serve with a straw or long handled spoon.

COFFEE MILK

(Recipe dated 1845)

1 dessert spoonful of ground coffee,
1 pint of milk,
2 shavings of isinglass.

" Boil the coffee, milk and isinglass together for a quarter of an hour. Allow this to stand for ten minutes, and pour the liquid off."

It might seem wise to sweeten this slightly, and as " isinglass " was the name applied to what we now know as " gelatine," would suggest that a teaspoonful of powdered gelatine would be a sufficient quantity to use.

COFFEE-MAPLE PUNCH

1 cupful of strong dripped coffee,
1½ pints of rich milk,
¼ cupful of maple syrup (4 tablespoonfuls),
1 egg,
Ice cream.

In making drip coffee, use recipe given under coffee recipes. Put the egg, two tablespoonfuls of cracked ice, the maple syrup, one cupful of milk and the egg in a shaker, shake thoroughly, strain into a pitcher, add the rest of the milk, and stir well. Pour into tall glasses, top with a tablespoonful of ice cream to each serving. Serve with a straw and a long handled spoon.

COFFEE-ROSE PUNCH

1 quart of milk,
1 cupful of strong dripped coffee,
½ cupful of plain syrup,
1 egg,
1 teaspoonful of rose extract,
Ice.

Put the coffee, ice, egg, syrup and a cupful of milk in a shaker. Shake thoroughly, pour into a pitcher, add the rest of the milk and the extract, stir well; fill tall thin glasses nearly full, add a tablespoonful of vanilla or rose ice cream and serve with a long handled spoon.

COFFEE MARSHMALLOW

1½ pints of milk,
1 cupful coffee,

⅓ cupful of plain syrup,
1 egg,
1 cupful of thick cream,
1 cupful of marshmallow cream,
    Ice.

Put one cupful of strong dripped coffee, one cupful of milk, the syrup, egg and ice in a shaker; shake thoroughly and pour into a pitcher. Add the rest of the milk, stir and pour into tall thin glasses, filling them three-quarters full. Whip the cream until stiff, mix with the marshmallow, and fill the glasses with the mixture. Top with a candied cherry if desired.

LEFT-OVER COCOA

Strain any cocoa left from breakfast or luncheon and place in the refrigerator until needed, either as a luncheon or afternoon drink.

Use parfait glasses, or any tall, narrow, stemmed glass. Pour into the glasses until about three-quarters full; add two tablespoonfuls of chocolate ice cream, top with marshmallow cream and a candied cherry. Serve with a long handled spoon and a straw.

If this is used in the afternoon, serve little cakes with it, being sure that the cakes do not have chocolate icing.

LEFT-OVER COFFEE

If there is one cupful of coffee left from the breakfast, put in the refrigerator until luncheon, or later in the afternoon.

1 cupful of coffee,
1 tablespoonful of plain syrup (see syrups),
1 pint of milk,
1 egg,
    Ice.

Put the egg, syrup, ice and coffee in a shaker, shake for

two minutes, pour into a glass pitcher with the milk, stir and serve at once.

EGG NOGG

½ pint of milk,
1 even teaspoonful of sugar,
1 egg,
¼ teaspoonful of vanilla extract,
  Ice,
  Nutmeg.

Break the egg into a cocktail shaker, add two table-spoonfuls of cracked ice, the milk, vanilla and sugar: shake thoroughly, strain into a tall thin glass, sprinkle with grated nutmeg and serve with a straw.

MILK SHAKE

½ pint of top milk,
1 teaspoonful of sugar,
¼ teaspoonful of vanilla,
  Ice,
  Nutmeg.

Put the milk, sugar, vanilla and two tablespoonfuls of cracked ice into a cocktail shaker; shake thoroughly and strain into a tall thin glass. Sprinkle grated nutmeg on top and serve.

RASPBERRY MILK SHAKE

½ pint of top milk,
¼ teaspoonful of sugar,
2 tablespoonfuls of raspberry syrup,
  Ice.

Put the top milk, or plain milk mixed with a little cream into a shaker with the sugar, syrup and two tablespoonfuls of cracked ice. Shake well for two minutes, strain into a tall thin glass. A tablespoonful of raspberry ice cream

is a desirable addition. Serve with a long handled spoon,
if the ice cream is used, or with a straw if not.

STRAWBERRY MILK SHAKE

½ pint of top milk,
½ teaspoonful of sugar,
2 tablespoonfuls of strawberry syrup,
   Ice.

Put the top milk, or plain milk mixed with a small amount
of cream into a cocktail shaker; add the sugar, strawberry
syrup, and two tablespoonfuls of cracked ice; shake well and
strain into a tall glass. If one wishes, a tablespoonful of
strawberry ice cream makes a delightful addition, as will
two selected strawberries, if in season.

CHOCOLATE MALTED MILK

2½ teaspoonfuls of malted milk,
 2 tablespoonfuls of chocolate syrup,
 1 cupful of milk,
   Ice.

Mix the malted milk with just enough hot water to blend
well, stirring and mixing with a spoon; add a little cold
milk to this, and pour it into a shaker. Add to this the
rest of the milk and the chocolate syrup and two tablespoonfuls of cracked ice. Shake well for two minutes.
Strain into a tall thin glass and serve.

CHOCOLATE MALTED MILK WITH EGG

2½ teaspoonfuls of malted milk,
 2 tablespoonfuls of chocolate syrup,
 1 cupful of milk,
 1 egg,
   Ice.

Mix the malted milk with only enough hot water to

make a paste; then add a little cold milk, enough to be able to pour the mixture. Pour into a shaker; add the egg, ice and chocolate syrup as well as the rest of the milk. Shake well for two minutes, and strain into a tall glass. A little sugar may be added if desired, although the syrup should make it sufficiently sweet.

RASPBERRY MALTED MILK

2½ teaspoonfuls of malted milk,
2 tablespoonfuls of raspberry syrup,
1 cupful of milk,
Ice.

Mix the malted milk with enough hot water to make a paste, stirring carefully to make sure that all the dry milk is blended, then add a little cold milk, stir well and pour into a cocktail shaker; add the rest of the milk, the raspberry syrup and two tablespoonfuls of ice. Shake well, strain into a tall glass and serve. If wished for, plain syrup or sugar may be added.

STRAWBERRY MALTED MILK WITH ICE CREAM

2½ teaspoonfuls of malted milk,
2 tablespoonfuls of strawberry syrup,
1 cupful of milk,
Ice.

Mix the malted milk with a little hot water, stirring until a smooth paste is made; add a little cold milk, stir again and pour into a shaker; add the rest of the milk and the strawberry syrup as well as two tablespoonfuls of cracked ice. Shake, strain into a tall glass. Top with a tablespoonful of ice cream, preferably vanilla.

VANILLA MALTED MILK WITH CHOCOLATE ICE CREAM

2½ teaspoonfuls of malted milk,
1 tablespoonful of plain syrup,

½ teaspoonful of vanilla extract,
1 cupful of rich milk,
  Ice,
  Ice cream.

Blend the malted milk with a little hot water, add enough cold milk to be able to pour it. Pour into a shaker, add the rest of the milk, plain syrup, vanilla and two tablespoonfuls of cracked ice. Shake well, strain into a tall thin glass and top with two tablespoonfuls of chocolate ice cream.

COFFEE MALTED MILK, EGG AND ICE CREAM

2½ teaspoonfuls of malted milk,
 2 tablespoonfuls of coffee syrup,
 1 cupful of rich milk,
 1 egg,
  Ice.

Blend the malted milk with a little hot water, being sure that the milk is well dissolved. Add enough cold milk to pour the mixture, and put it in a cocktail shaker with the rest of the milk, the coffee syrup, egg and ice. Shake for two minutes, and strain into a tall thin glass and top with two tablespoonfuls of vanilla ice cream.

There surely is nourishment enough in this for a normal luncheon.

COFFEE MALTED MILK

1½ teaspoonfuls of malted milk,
 1 tablespoonful of plain syrup,
 2 tablespoonfuls of coffee syrup,
  Ice.

Mix the malted milk with a little hot water, blending it well, add enough cold milk to make thin enough to pour; pour into a cocktail shaker and add the rest of the milk, the coffee syrup and two tablespoonfuls of cracked ice.

Shake hard for two minutes; strain into an attractive glass and serve.

MALTED EGG-MILK

2½ teaspoonfuls of malted milk,
1 teaspoonful of sugar,
1 cupful of rich milk,
2 tablespoonfuls of ice,
½ teaspoonful of vanilla extract,
1 egg.

Put the malted milk in a cup, add sugar and mix with just enough hot water to dissolve the malted milk, stirring and mixing with a spoon. Add a little cold milk, stir well, and pour into a cocktail shaker with the rest of the milk, the egg, ice and the vanilla. Shake this mixture thoroughly, strain into a tall thin glass and serve.

GRENADINE MILK SHAKE

⅛ cupful of grenadine (2 tablespoonfuls),
1 egg,
1 cupful of rich milk,
  Ice,
  Nutmeg.

Put the egg, milk, grenadine and ice in a shaker and shake thoroughly; shaking hard for at least two minutes. Strain into a tall glass, and sprinkle with grated nutmeg.

MILK APPLEBLOOM

¼ cupful of sparkling apple juice (commercial) (4 table-
    spoonfuls),
1 teaspoonful of sugar,
1 cupful of milk,
½ teaspoonful of Florida water,
  Ice.

Put the apple juice, ice, sugar and Florida water in a

shaker, shake well; open the shaker and add the milk, again shaking well. Strain into an attractive glass and serve at once.

ORANGE MILK

1 orange,
1 teaspoonful of sugar,
1 cupful of milk,
¼ teaspoonful of orange extract,
  Nutmeg,
  Ice.

Extract the juice from the orange and put it with the ice, sugar and orange extract into a shaker and shake well for two minutes. Remove the top, add the milk, pouring slowly and stirring at the same time, then recap the shaker and shake thoroughly again. Strain into a tall glass and sprinkle with nutmeg. Serve at once.

EGG SNOWDRIFT

1 egg,
½ pint of milk (1 cupful),
1 teaspoonful of sugar,
¼ teaspoonful of vanilla,
  Nutmeg.

Separate the white and yolk of the egg, whip the white until stiff, sweeten slightly with powdered sugar. Put the sugar, vanilla and a tablespoonful of milk with the yolks, beat this with a whisk until light and lemon colored; stir in the rest of the milk; pour this mixture into a tall glass, and add the slightly sweetened white, piling it high. Sprinkle with grated nutmeg and serve with a straw.

SILLABUB

1 pint of thick cream,
1 cupful of powdered sugar,
¼ cupful of raspberry juice.

It is quite possible in most large places to purchase a
sillabub churn, which is a small tin cylinder, having a small
dasher which fits loosely.

Whip the cream until frothy, using the churn; sweeten
to taste with the powdered sugar and add the raspberry
juice, which should be stirred in swiftly and the drink
served at once in tall, stemmed glasses. Serve with long
handled spoons.

If a churn is not obtainable, use a cream whisk, but stop
beating at the frothy stage.

SILLABUB WITH GRAPE JUICE

1 quart of thick cream,
4 egg whites,
1 cupful of grape juice,
1¾ cupfuls of powdered sugar,

Whip the cream until very stiff, adding half the powdered
sugar; whip the egg whites until dry, adding remaining
sugar gradually; when finished, mix the cream and the
beaten whites thoroughly and add the grape juice. Eat
with a spoon and serve in low wide glasses.

CANTON MILK SHAKE

½ pint of top milk,
1 egg,
1 inch preserved ginger,
1 tablespoonful of plain syrup,
  Ice.

Chop half the ginger very fine; put it with the top
milk, syrup, ice and the yolk of the egg into a cocktail shaker
and shake for two minutes. Whip the white of the egg until
stiff; cut the remaining half inch of ginger into small pieces.
Strain the milk mixture into a tall glass, reserving a quarter
cupful; mix this quickly with the beaten white, add to the

mixture in the glass and top with the small pieces of ginger. Serve with a straw and a long handled spoon.

VICHY AND MILK

¾ cupful of rich milk,
  Vichy.

Pour three-quarters cupful of rich milk in an iced tea glass and fill with vichy.

Physicians order this for patients who cannot take, or who do not like milk plain, and find that in most cases the patient can take it.

MILK AND VICHY WITH SYRUP

¾ cupful of milk,
2 tablespoonfuls of raspberry syrup (home-made or commercial),
  Vichy.

Pour the syrup into a tall glass (iced tea glass is the right size) and add the milk; stir well and fill the glass with vichy. The raspberry syrup will disguise both the milk taste and the vichy, in case one does not like either.

HOT MILK DRINKS

HOT MILK

For the person who is tired and who does not like plain cold milk, try heating the milk until just below the boiling point, adding a goodly sized pinch of salt and a generous sprinkling of paprika. Serve with a saltine or a toasted cracker.

HOT MILK WITH CELERY SALT

Heat the milk until just below the boiling point, add a generous pinch of salt and a sprinkling of celery salt; stir well and serve with toasted crackers.

HOT MALTED MILK

2 teaspoonfuls of malted milk,
1 teaspoonful of sugar,
⅛ teaspoonful of salt,
1 cupful of milk.

Blend the malted milk with enough hot water to make it smooth, add the salt and sugar, stirring thoroughly and add the cupful of milk, which should have been heated until just below the boiling point.

HOT MALTED MILK WITH CHOCOLATE

2 teaspoonfuls of malted milk,
2 tablespoonfuls of chocolate syrup,
1 cupful of milk.

Blend the malted milk with a little hot water; stir until smooth; add the chocolate syrup, stir, and add the milk which should be heated until just before the boiling point is reached.

HOT MALTED MILK WITH COFFEE

2 teaspoonfuls of malted milk,
2 tablespoonfuls of strong dripped coffee,
2 teaspoonfuls of sugar,
1 cupful of milk.

Blend the malted milk with enough hot water to make smooth, add the sugar and stir until well mixed, add the coffee and the milk heated until the boiling point is reached.

Coffee syrup may be used if desired. Use two tablespoonfuls, but do not use sugar with it.

BUTTERMILK

Buttermilk as a beverage is to be greatly desired because of its food value as well as the fact that it is a most refreshing drink.

The food content is very high, having nearly all the food materials found in whole milk, excepting, of course, the butter fats, which have been removed by churning; still some fats do remain; especially is this true of buttermilk obtained direct from such farmers as do not use the most advanced methods of butter-making.

We find 3 per cent. of protein, nearly 5 per cent. of carbohydrates in the form of milk sugar, 0.7 per cent. of mineral constituents, and about 0.5 per cent. of fats.

Buttermilk is recommended by many successful physicians as an aid in intestinal disorders.

Buttermilk is served at most soda fountains, and may be ordered from one's dairyman, also may be obtained at some grocers' and at all better class hotels.

BUTTERMILK LEMONADE

For persons not caring for buttermilk plain, one may make a lemonade which is healthful as well as delicious.

1 quart of buttermilk,
2 lemons,
2 tablespoonfuls of sugar.

Extract the juice of the lemons, add the sugar and stir until dissolved; add the buttermilk, stirring constantly. If a smaller quantity is to be made it were well to use a shaker, for then the lemonade will be so thoroughly mixed that the results will be most satisfactory.

"LACTO"

The following recipe is taken from a bulletin issued by the Iowa Agricultural Experiment Station.

2 quarts of buttermilk,
2 pounds of sugar,
2 eggs,
1¾ cupfuls of orange juice,
¼ cupful of lemon juice.

Dissolve the sugar in the buttermilk and add the eggs, yolks and whites beaten separately. Stir and strain the mixture and add the fruit juices. Freeze as for ice cream, and pack in ice for an hour before serving.

VIII — COFFEE, CHOCOLATE, COCOA AND TEA

A book of beverage recipes which did not give directions for making coffee, tea and cocoa would surely fail in its mission.

I have given recipes from many countries, and by many men famous for coffee making, feeling sure that each reader will find the exact one to please the fancy of himself or herself and family.

COFFEE

Even though we as Americans are coffee drinkers to almost an alarming degree, it is not often that we find a cook who really makes excellent coffee.

When purchasing coffee one must be influenced by one's taste; whether all Java, whether equal parts of Mocha and Java, or whether a blend of one's own or a commercial blend is used.

One thing should be remembered, and that is: good coffee is served as soon as it is made.

The pot should always be hot before the coffee is made.

The late Francis B. Thurber, a coffee importer, who made coffee a study both as it came to this country and as it was grown in its native state, gives the following recipe as his idea of unexcelled coffee:

To one cupful of coffee ground moderately fine add one egg with shell, and enough cold water to wet the grounds. Pour on one pint of boiling water and let it boil for fifteen minutes. Remove the pot from the fire and allow it to stand for three minutes to settle, then strain into a warm coffee pot. Serve in cups half filled with boiling milk, or if cream is used dilute with hot water.

FRENCH DRIP COFFEE

For *cafe noir* use two tablespoonfuls of finely ground coffee for each cup. Coffee should be packed tightly as possible in the upper part of the French pot, and the boiling water poured through. When this has dripped through, redrip and serve.

Parisian housekeepers, before throwing out the grounds, pour boiling water through the coffee again, reserving this for use the next time coffee is made.

Much of the flavor of French coffee is said to be due to this practice.

VIENNA COFFEE

The pot required to make coffee after this method is the style with a cloth bag in the top.

Use two level tablespoonfuls of coffee to the cup, and place in the bag, pouring the boiling water through.

Serve with hot milk.

ENGLISH COFFEE

After the recipe of M. Soyer, a former *chef* of the Savoy.

Place two ounces of moderately fine ground coffee in a stew-pan, and without adding water, hold over the fire, stirring with a spoon until the coffee is very hot. Pour over the coffee a pint of boiling water and cover closely; remove at once from fire and let stand for five minutes, then strain through a cloth, heat and serve with or without cream.

COFFEE, BRAZILIAN STYLE

In Brazil, whence practically all of the world's supply of coffee comes, the popular method is to place the coffee in a *woolen* bag, which is placed in a pot and boiling water poured over it. The coffee is immediately poured off.

COFFEE, BATAVIA STYLE

(As made by the Dutch coffee planters in Java)

The coffee is ground fine and packed tightly in the top of a French pot.   The required amount of *cold* water is poured over it and allowed to drip through.   It requires about five hours for the process if the coffee is packed as tightly as it should be.   The coffee is then heated and from three to four times its volume of hot milk added.

TURKISH COFFEE

A heaping dessertspoonful of powdered coffee is added to one small cupful of cold water.   This is brought to a boil, and the coffee and grounds are poured into the cup.

Turkish coffee is drunk grounds and all, without cream or sugar.

KAFFEE "KULTUR"

It is the unanimous observation of civilized travelers that good coffee is unobtainable in Germany.   The foremost scientist of that race, the famous Baron von Liebig, nearly a hundred years ago wrote an exhaustive treatise on the subject of coffee and coffee-making, and devised the concoction which among Germans now passes for coffee.   Was it not given them by authority?   This is von Liebig's recipe:

Put three-quarters of the amount of coffee to be used on the fire in boiling water; boil from ten to fifteen minutes. Then put in the remaining one-quarter of the coffee, cover and let it stand for five minutes.   Stir, strain and serve with an equal amount of milk.

EXCELLENT COFFEE

Use a drip pot, one having a cloth bag.   Wet the bag, place the coffee in this, and pack as tightly as possible around the sides and bottom.   Pour in slowly three cupfuls of boiling water to each half cupful of powdered coffee. Place the pot on the back of the range, or on an asbestos mat with only enough flame under to keep it warm, and pour the water slowly.

Serve with cream as soon as dripped.

TEA

Chin Hung, Chinese scholar and philosopher, to whom all the agricultural and medical knowledge of China is traced, once said, so I am told: "Tea is better than wine, for it leadeth not to intoxication, neither does it cause a man to say foolish things. It is better than water, for it doth not carry disease, neither doth it act as poison."

There are really but two kinds of teas on the market: green and black. The color of the tea depends on the oxidation; black tea being exposed to the air, or oxidized before final drying, while green tea is dried immediately after rolling.

There are a number of different brands with which we are all familiar, such as Formosa, Oolong, Ceylon, English Breakfast, Orange Pekoe, and Flowery Pekoe.

Right here I will say that if a spray of orange blossom is kept in the tea caddy one need not pay the price for Orange Pekoe.

TEA MAKING

Be sure that the water is boiling, and use it at once. Rinse the pot with hot water. Place the tea in the pot in a "ball," and pour over the freshly boiled water, allowing it to stand for five minutes, then the tea-ball and the tea should be removed.

Use a level teaspoonful of tea to one and a half cupfuls of water. I think most people will want to dilute this, even.

RUSSIAN TEA

"Russian tea" has a rather inflated reputation, and is not really known in this country as it is used there.

A great amount of tea infusion is used, as the samovar is always in evidence, but the water is poured on the tea again and again, making a great amount of liquid without much strength. Sugar and lemon juice is added and it is drunk from a glass.

ICED TEA

One may make fresh tea and pour it over cracked ice in individual glasses, or one may make a rather strong solution of tea, and add cracked ice to it in a large pitcher, or make a weaker solution, and pour over cracked ice in glasses. The method must depend upon the fancy of one's family, or the hostess.

ICED TEA WITH MINT

While iced tea is usually served with sugar and lemon, I am quite sure that in addition a spray of mint will be found most acceptable. Place the mint in the glass and pour the tea over.

HOT TEA WITH MINT

I find that a cupful of hot tea into which a few leaves of mint have been placed is most refreshing. This may be served either with or without sugar.

COCOA AND CHOCOLATE

It is very rare for one to serve chocolate these days, as cocoa in a perfected form is put up by reliable firms in this country, and most hostesses prefer it to chocolate, which is more difficult to prepare and rather richer than wise to serve to the family generally.

COCOA

1 cupful of milk,
1 teaspoonful of cocoa.

Bring the milk to the boiling point and pour in the cocoa moistened with a little warm water. Stir and allow to boil, beating with a cream whip for a minute or two. Pour through a strainer into a cup or individual pot. Multiply this amount by the number of cups to be served.

COCOA No. 2

1 cupful of milk,
2 teaspoonfuls of cocoa.

Use a *porcelain* kettle; mix the cocoa with enough hot water to make a smooth paste, pour the milk over it slowly, mixing constantly, so that there will be no lumps left undissolved. Bring to the boiling point, and boil for ten minutes. Strain, and serve at once. A teaspoonful of sweetened whipped cream added to each cup adds perceptibly to the acceptability. Sweeten to taste.

CHOCOLATE

2 cupfuls of milk,
2 tablespoonfuls of grated chocolate.

Grate enough unsweetened chocolate to make two tablespoonfuls, mix with a little boiling water, and melt slowly over a low fire, then add the milk, pouring carefully, stirring while pouring. Allow this to boil for ten minutes and strain. Whipped cream added to each serving is delightful, although it makes the drink a bit too rich for most people. It would be unadvisable for persons given to stoutness to drink chocolate.

CHOCOLATE

(Recipe of 1845)

1 inch of a cake of chocolate,
1 quart of boiling water,
Milk.

Shave the chocolate fine, pour on the boiling water; boil for twenty minutes, add milk to please and boil up again. Serve.

CHOCOLATE (CRÉOLE RECIPE)

1 cake of French chocolate,
1 quart of milk,

Grate the chocolate; mix with a little hot water, and stir into the milk which should have reached the simmering stage.   Stir until the mixture boils; allow it to boil up once, and serve immediately.   This may be sweetened after serving or allow two tablespoonfuls of sugar to the full amount.   Add whipped cream if desired.

COCOA (CRÉOLE RECIPE)

4 tablespoonfuls of cocoa,
1 quart of milk.

Put the milk in a double boiler; moisten the cocoa with a little milk, and pour into the milk as it begins to boil, stirring constantly.   Let it boil up once, only, and serve. Whipped cream may be used with it if desired.

COCOA (OLD NEW ENGLAND RECIPE)

2 tablespoonfuls of cocoa,
1 quart of water,
1½ cupfuls of milk.

Mix the cocoa with a little water and pour into the full amount of water and allow to boil for a half hour, skim, add the milk and allow it to boil up again.   Serve.

IX — DRINKS FOR INVALIDS AND SMALL CHILDREN

I shall try to give a few helpful suggestions in this chapter for the making of drinks which are both appetizing and nutritious. Some are offered because of their nutritive value and some, like treacle, posset and Iceland moss, because they are a real aid in helping to ward off colds and some because they please the palate of the invalid or the child whose appetite must be catered to.

APPLE WATER

2 large tart apples,
1 tablespoonful of lemon juice,
1 pint of boiling water,
  Lemon peel,
  Sugar.

Peel, core and slice the apples; place them in a deep bowl with the lemon juice, one strip of rind and as much sugar as the nurse or mother thinks wise, and cover with the boiling water, allowing this to stand covered tightly until cold. Strain, chill and serve in small glasses. Be sure to serve on a plate on which a fresh doylie is placed.

APPLE TEA (FROM ROAST APPLES)

(Very old recipe)

3 apples,
  Pint of water.

Roast sour apples until tender, pour boiling water over them and let them stand until cold. Sweeten a little if the patient so desires.

APPLE TEA (UP-STATE RECIPE)

3 large tart apples,
1 pint of water,
  Sugar.

Peel and slice the apples very thin, pour a pint of boiling water over them and boil for five minutes. Allow them to stand until cold, then strain off the water. Sweeten it slightly, unless the patient prefers the water very tart.

ARROWROOT WITH MILK

½ pint of milk,
1 dessertspoonful of arrowroot,
1 teaspoonful of sugar.

Mix the arrowroot with a little cold milk until a smooth paste. Pour a half pint of boiled milk over it, pouring slowly and stirring constantly. Bring to the boiling point and boil for six minutes. (Arrowroot *must* be well boiled). Strain, add the sugar and serve.

I want to impress upon my readers the necessity of serving any drink intended for an invalid in the most attractive manner possible.

ARROWROOT WITH WATER

½ pint of water,
1 dessertspoonful of arrowroot,
1 teaspoonful of sugar,
1 teaspoonful of lemon juice.

Mix the arrowroot with a little cold water, making it perfectly smooth. Pour the boiling water over this slowly, stirring well; cook until boiling, and continue for six minutes. Strain, add sugar and lemon juice. Serve in an attractive glass on a pretty plate on which a spotless doylie is laid.

BARLEY WATER

Many cannot take milk plain, but the addition of barley water adds to its digestibility.

2 ounces of pearl barley,
1 pint of water,
  Sugar.

Pour the water over the barley and boil slowly until there is a third less liquid. Strain and add sugar and serve. Barley water may be served alone or with milk. It is more palatable with milk.

BARLEY WATER MADE FROM BARLEY FLOUR

1 teaspoonful of barley flour,
½ pint of water,
1 pinch of salt.

Mix the barley flour with a little cold water, making a smooth paste; pour the rest of the water on slowly, mixing and stirring constantly. Boil for a half hour, boiling fast all the time. Strain and add to milk, or add a little sugar, or if it is for an infant, it may be given from a nursing bottle without the sugar, between feedings, especially if the child is not getting sufficient nourishment from its own food.

BLACK CURRANT TEA

It is said that this tea is excellent to alleviate hoarseness, and is a most appetizing beverage.

1 dessertspoonful of black currant jam,
½ pint of water,
1 teaspoonful of sugar.

Put jam, sugar and water in an enamel dish and bring to the boiling point; simmer for five or six minutes. Strain and add lemon juice and serve hot; or chill and add a little cracked ice and serve very cold.

BRAN TEA

2 tablespoonfuls of bran,
1 pint of water,
½ ounce of gum arabic,
1 tablespoonful of honey.

Mix water and bran and boil for fifteen minutes. Add gum arabic and honey, stir until dissolved. Strain through a cloth and serve. This, too, may be served hot or cold.

EGG WHITE AND MILK (ENGLISH RECIPE)

1 egg white,
1 cupful of milk,
  Vanilla.

Boil the milk and let it cool. Whip the egg white until dry and put it in a tall glass with the milk, flavor with vanilla and serve.

OLD FASHIONED CAUDLE (ENGLISH)

1 tablespoonful of fine oatmeal (ground, not rolled),
1 cupful of water,
1 cupful of milk,
1 tablespoonful of lemon juice,
1 strip of lemon rind,
1 tablespoonful of sugar,
  Nutmeg.

Boil oatmeal, water, milk and lemon rind together for ten minutes; remove the rind, add the lemon juice, sugar and a sprinkling of grated nutmeg. Serve hot. The beaten yolk of an egg may be stirred in if extra nourishment is needed.

CAUDLE (OLD NEW ENGLAND RECIPE)

1 pint of rice gruel (see gruel),
1 egg yolk,
1 tablespoonful of sugar,

¼ cupful of cold water,
2 tablespoonfuls of orange juice,
1 teaspoonful of lemon juice,
   Nutmeg.

When the gruel is boiling, add the following mixture; beat the yolk of the egg with the sugar and stir in the water, fruit juices and a sprinkling of grated nutmeg. Strain and serve very hot.

CREAM AND CARBONATED WATER

¼ cupful of cream,
   Carbonated water.

There are times when a patient is not allowed milk, but cream is permissible; under those conditions, this will be found useful as well as nutritious.

Pour the cream in a tumbler or straight-sided, tall glass; fill the glass with carbonated water, using a syphon.

MILK AND CARBONATED WATER

¼ cupful of carbonated water,
¾ cupful of milk.

It is a matter of taste just what carbonated water one uses: whether seltzer, vichy or club soda; whether poured from a bottle or a syphon. Put the milk in a tall glass and fill with the carbonated water.

EGG WHITE, LEMON AND CARBONATED WATER

1 egg white,
1 tablespoonful of lemon juice,
   Carbonated water.

Beat the white of the egg until stiff, put it in a tall glass and add the lemon juice; fill the glass with the carbonated water.

EGG YOLK, LEMON JUICE AND CARBONATED WATER

1 egg yolk,
1 tablespoonful of lemon juice,
   Carbonated water.

Beat the yolk until lemon colored, pour into a tumbler and stir in the lemon juice. Fill the glass with the carbonated water.

EGG WHITE AND ORANGE JUICE

1 egg white,
1 cupful of orange juice.

Extract the juice from enough oranges (two Florida oranges will usually prove sufficient) ; strain into a tall glass ; whip the egg white until stiff, and stir it into the orange juice.

If the patient does not like the taste of the egg white, it were well to beat the white until stiff, put it in a cocktail shaker with the orange juice, shake well for a minute or two and strain into a glass. It will be so blended that it will be very difficult to taste anything excepting the orange juice.

EGG WHITE, ORANGE JUICE AND CARBONATED WATER

1 egg white,
1 orange,
   Carbonated water.

Beat the white until stiff ; extract the juice from the orange, stir the egg in carefully and pour into a tall glass. Fill the glass with carbonated water.

EGG WHITE, ORANGE JUICE AND DISTILLED WATER

1 egg white,
1 tablespoonful of orange juice,
2 tablespoonfuls of distilled water.

If a baby is very ill and cannot retain food, this will tide it over until a physician can be called and prescribe.

Beat the egg white until stiff, stir in the orange juice and then the water. Feed with a spoon.

FLAXSEED TEA

2 tablespoonfuls of whole flaxseed,
1 pint of water,
1 lemon,
2 tablespoonfuls of granulated sugar.

Mix the flaxseed with a little water, adding the remainder of the pint and boil for fifteen minutes. Slice a lemon in a deep bowl and add two tablespoonfuls of granulated sugar. Strain the flaxseed tea boiling hot, over this, stir and allow to stand until cold. Strain again and use in tablespoonful doses. This is used for cold or to relieve an irritated throat.

GRUEL (ENGLISH RECIPE)

½ pint of milk or water,
1 dessertspoonful of fine oatmeal (ground, not rolled),
    Salt or sugar.

Mix the oatmeal with a little cold water in an enameled saucepan; add the milk or water boiling hot, and boil for ten minutes, stirring constantly. Strain, pressing as much of the oatmeal through the sieve as possible. Add either salt or sugar as the patient desires. As gruel induces perspiration it is best to take it after one is in bed. This is most satisfactory as an aid in breaking up a cold.

INDIAN MEAL GRUEL (YELLOW CORN MEAL)

2 teaspoonfuls of ground Indian corn meal,
½ pint of water,
    Sugar,
    Nutmeg,
    Cream.

Mix the corn meal with enough cold water to make a smooth paste; add a pint of water, bring to the boiling point and boil slowly for one half hour,— never less; strain, add a little salt, or a little sugar if the patient does not like the salt. If sugar is used add a sprinkling of grated nutmeg, if salt is preferred, add two tablespoonfuls of cream; stir and serve at once.

OATMEAL GRUEL

4 tablespoonfuls of oatmeal (ground, not rolled),
3 pints of water,
⅓ cupful of raisins,
  Salt,
  Sugar.

Wet the oatmeal with a little cold water, pour over it three pints of boiling water, and boil gently for two hours. Strain, add a sprinkle of salt and enough sugar to satisfy the patient. A very little mace or nutmeg may be added, and, if one wishes, a half cupful of raisins may be put in as soon as the boiling point is reached. If raisins are used it is not at all necessary to use sugar, for there is plenty of sugar in them to make the gruel most palatable.

RICE GRUEL

2 teaspoonfuls of ground rice,
½ pint of water,
  Salt,
  Cream (if allowed).

Blend the rice with a little cold water, add the half pint of boiling water and boil for five minutes. Season with a little salt, and if allowed add three tablespoonfuls of thick cream, or if milk is preferred use that.

POTATO GRUEL (ENGLISH RECIPE)

2 large potatoes,
  Milk.

Steam two large mealy or floury potatoes, press through a fine sieve, and add hot milk slowly, stirring and blending until the consistency of thin cream. Salt to taste and serve.

CARROT GRUEL

2 large, or 4 small carrots,
Milk.

Boil the carrots until very tender, press through a fine sieve and add hot milk slowly, being sure to mix well and smoothly. When the consistency of cream is reached, add a little salt and serve.

An English physician recommends this as an aid in treating scurvy in children.

IRISH OR ICELAND MOSS

½ ounce of Irish moss,
1 pint of water,
Lemon juice,
Sugar.

Wash the moss, put it in a covered dish and allow it to stand in enough water to cover over night. Throw off this water and cover with a pint of fresh water; simmer for one hour, strain, add a tablespoonful of lemon juice and a little sugar, being sure that it is not too sweet.

Irish moss is a sea weed and is rather rich in mucilage, iodine and sulphur, and is given as an aid in treatment for colds, especially when there is a cough.

HOME MADE KOUMISS

(Recipe from an English Physician)

Boil fresh milk, and when nearly cold put into quart bottles, leaving room to shake. Add ½ ounce of crushed lump sugar, a very small piece of compressed yeast — about

one twenty-fourth of the ordinary yeast cake — cork, tie
down the cork unless a patent stopper is used; lay the bottles on the side, and shake twice daily. If the weather is
hot this may be used on the fifth day, if cool, on the sixth,
if very cold, on the seventh.

LINSEED TEA

1 ounce of whole linseed,
½ pint of water,
¼ ounce of liquorice,
¼ ounce of rock candy,
½ lemon.

Wash the linseed and simmer with the lemon rind and
water for a half hour. Take from the fire, add liquorice
and rock candy and stir until dissolved. Strain and add
the lemon juice. Useful in treatment of colds.

PRUNE TEA

2 ounces of prunes,
1 pint of boiling water,
1 teaspoonful of lemon juice.

Be sure to select California prunes, for then no sugar will
be needed.

Wash the prunes and put in a saucepan with the water;
simmer for an hour, cut the prunes while in the water, then
strain through a fine sieve, pressing some of the pulp
through. Add the lemon juice and serve to the patient in a
wine glass. This is excellent in cases of constipation.

RICE WATER

1 ounce of best Sea Island rice,
1 quart of water,
  Salt.

There is no better rice grown than that which we get from

the islands which lie in the Atlantic off the state of South Carolina. This is large full rice and is by far the most desirable for use for invalids and children.

Wash the rice in cold water, rubbing it well between the hands. Allow water to run over it until the water runs clear. Throw the washed rice in a quart of cold water, and cook rapidly until it boils hard. Then cook slower over a lower fire until rather mushy. Two hours is not too long for the boiling. Strain through a fine sieve. Add a little salt, or if the patient greatly prefers, and sugar will not harm, sweeten slightly.

This is used in cases of dysentery with salt only, as a drink.

RICE MILK

1 ounce of rice (Sea Island),
1 pint of milk,
  Salt or sugar.

Wash the rice as directed in the foregoing recipe, and put into a saucepan with the milk. Boil for one hour. Add salt to taste or a very little sugar. The salt is preferable. Do not strain this.

TOAST WATER

1 full sized crust of bread,
1 pint of water.

Select the crust of the bread, cut at least an inch thick; toast or dry it until brown in the oven, being sure that it does not burn or scorch, but is thoroughly brown. Put this in a deep bowl and pour one pint of cold water over it, allowing it to stand for one hour. Strain and use. One may season with a little salt or a sprinkling of celery salt. It may be served either hot or cold.

TREACLE (MOLASSES) POSSET

(English recipe)

½ pint of milk,
2 tablespoonfuls of molasses,
¼ lemon.

Put the milk into a saucepan, and bring to the boiling point; add the molasses and lemon juice. This will curdle. Strain through a fine cloth. Use hot or cold.

THICK MILK

½ ounce of baked flour,
½ pint of milk,
  Sugar.

Put a half ounce of flour in a dish and put into the oven, allowing it to brown slightly. Blend it with the milk, stirring a few drops of milk into the flour at a time, until all the milk is used. Boil for five minutes, stirring constantly. Sweeten a trifle and use.

This is given to patients at times when they are on a liquid diet and a change is needed. A little nutmeg will again change the taste.

LEMON WHEY

½ pint of milk,
½ lemon,
  Sugar.

Boil the milk and add the juice from a half lemon. It will, of course, curdle. Strain through a fine cloth; sweeten slightly and use.

MILK WHEY

(English recipe)

1 pint of sweet milk,
½ pint of buttermilk.

Bring the milk to the boiling point, add the buttermilk and boil for a minute. Strain and use.

MEAT BROTHS AND TEAS

BEEF TEA OR BROTH

½ pound of beef,
¼ teaspoonful of salt,
½ pint of water.

Select a piece of beef which has little or no fat, preferably from the top round; remove any fats, and cut into strips, then cut across, shredding the meat. Put the shredded meat, salt and *cold* water in an enamel saucepan and allow it to soak for fifteen minutes, then place over a slow fire. Cook until the meat is white and the juice or broth a deep red-brown. Strain through a fine strainer, pressing the beef hard. Remove any particles of grease by drawing a piece of brown paper over the top. Serve hot. Be sure to serve in an attractive cup on a doylie. Please the eye and the appetite is more likely to be tempted.

BEEF TEA (MADE IN A JAR)

1 pound of top round,
1 pint of cold water,
½ teaspoonful of salt.

Remove the fat, shred the meat finely and put into a glass jar. A two quart glass can such as is used for preserving is desirable. Fasten the cover, whether a screw-top or patent fastener, and place in a deep pan of boiling water. Keep the water simmering for at least three hours. Stir the beef occasionally. Strain and remove any fat by drawing a paper over the top. Serve.

BEEF TEA (RAW BEEF)

2 ounces of top round,
2 tablespoonfuls of cold water,
  Pinch of salt.

Cut all the fat and skin from the beef, and cut into shreds;
place in a glass dish with the water and salt, cover and place
in a cold place and allow to stand for two hours.   Strain
and press out all the juice possible.   Serve a teaspoonful
or two at a time.   This will not keep, so only a very small
amount should be made at a time.

BEEF EXTRACT (RAW)

½ pound of top round,
  Salt.

This extract is given when nourishment must be pushed
and can only be given in small quantities.   It is invaluable in
cases of rickets and scurvy in children.

There are small meat presses on the market, which are
made for the purpose of extracting the blood and may be
purchased at any large department store where there is a
housekeeping department.

Put the meat in a pan and sear it quickly; then cut into
small pieces and place in the meat press; by turning the
screw-top extract the blood or juice, and pour into a glass.
After all the blood is extracted, salt slightly and feed with a
spoon.

BEEF TEA WITH EGG

½ pint of beef tea,
1 egg yolk,
  Salt.

Beat the egg yolk until a light yellow and stir into a half
cupful of hot beef tea.   Add a trifle of salt if necessary.

BEEF TEA FOR CONVALESCENTS

1 pound of top round,
1 pint of water,
1 piece of carrot,
1 piece of turnip,
1 spray of parsley,
1 tiny pinch of thyme,
   Small slice of onion,
   Salt.

Remove all fat from the meat, cut the vegetables into tiny pieces, shred the meat and put all in a glass jar with the herbs and salt. Fasten the top and place in a deep pan nearly full of hot water and cook slowly for three hours. Strain and remove any fat which may have been left.

MUTTON TEA

½ pound of lean mutton,
½ pint of water,
¼ teaspoonful of salt.

Select the juicy part of the neck, remove as much fat as possible, cut into tiny pieces, put into a saucepan with cold water and salt. Simmer gently until the meat turns white and the tea or broth a rich red-brown. Strain, remove all fat by passing a paper over the top. If it is not possible to remove the fat in this way, cool the broth and remove the fat, then reheat. To reheat place the dish holding the broth in a pan of hot water. Do not allow broths or teas to boil.

CHICKEN BROTH

½ chicken (small fowl is as desirable as a chicken),
1 quart of water,
1 tablespoonful of rice,
½ teaspoonful of chopped parsley,
¼ teaspoonful of salt.

Cut the chicken into small pieces, and break the bones.

Put the meat and bones into a saucepan with the cold water, salt and rice. (The rice may be omitted if preferred.) Simmer for three hours, strain, sprinkle with parsley and serve.

This broth may be made leaving the rice out until cooked, then strain, return to the saucepan, reheat to the boiling point, add the rice and cook for twenty-five minutes. It depends entirely on whether the patient may have the rice whole or cooked soft enough to pass through a fine sieve.

MUTTON BROTH (WITH BARLEY)

1 pound of mutton (neck or breast),
1 quart of water,
1 tablespoonful of barley (pearl),
  Salt,
  Chopped parsley.

Remove all fats possible and cut the mutton into small pieces. Put into the saucepan with the *cold* water and salt, bring to the boiling point, skim, add the barley and simmer for three hours. Strain and sprinkle with the chopped parsley. If this broth is intended for a convalescent, it need not be strained; remove the meat and bones only, leaving the well cooked barley.

OYSTER BROTH

6 selected oysters,
½ cupful of milk or broth,
1 tablespoonful of cream.

Put the oysters, their liquor, and the milk or broth (preferably the milk) in a saucepan, and bring to the boiling point. Simmer for *one minute,* and strain. The oysters may be chopped finely and returned to the broth or not, as liked. It would seem wise in most instances to remove the beards and gristle first and chop only the soft parts.

CLAM BROTH

Scrub the clams in cold water and place over a hot fire in a large kettle and heat until the shells open. Place two thicknesses of cheese cloth over a deep dish and strain. Season the broth and serve.

CLAM JUICE (COMMERCIAL)

There is a clam juice on the market,— a " clam concentrate "— which makes a satisfactory broth if it is not possible to obtain fresh clams.

1 teaspoonful of concentrated clam juice,
½ cupful of boiling water,
   Seasoning to suit.

Put the concentrated juice in a cup and pour the boiling water over it, stirring until well mixed. Season to taste.

One may use milk if one wishes instead of water, or may use half water and half milk.

COMMERCIAL BEEF TEA OR BROTH

There are several manufacturers who put out concentrated beef extracts, some in cubes, and some in a sort of paste form. If one uses the cubes, one cube is used to each three-quarters of a cupful of boiling water. Season with salt, or with salt and celery salt.

If one wishes, a drop or two of onion juice may be added to this beef tea, as well as salt and celery salt.

X — MISCELLANEOUS DRINKS

I shall give under this heading several drinks which do not seem to fit in any other place.

GENERAL HARRISON'S EGG NOGG

1 egg,
½ teaspoonful of sugar,
¼ cupful of crushed ice,
⅝ cupful of sweet cider.

Place all the ingredients in a cocktail shaker and shake well for two minutes. Strain into a tall, straight-sided glass and sprinkle with grated nutmeg.

SARATOGA COOLER

1 teaspoonful of powdered sugar,
½ lemon,
½ pint of ginger ale,
  Ice.

Put the sugar and lemon juice in a tall glass, stir until the sugar is dissolved; add two or three pieces of ice, and pour over this a bottle of ginger ale. Stir and remove the ice. Serve.

SODA NECTAR

1 lemon,
1 cupful of water,
1 teaspoonful of powdered sugar,
½ teaspoonful of bicarbonate of soda,
  Ice.

Put a cupful of water in an iced tea glass, strain the juice of a lemon into it; add the sugar and stir well until the sugar is dissolved. Put in two tablespoonfuls of cracked ice, and stir until very cold, then stir in the soda. As soon as it begins to effervesce, serve it.

NECTAR FOR DOG DAYS

(Recipe by a famous mixer of drinks)

1 lemon,
1 bottle of club soda,
  Ice.

Strain the juice of the lemon into a tall glass, add two tablespoonfuls of cracked ice and pour the soda over it. Serve at once.

SNOW BALL

½ teaspoonful of powdered sugar,
1 egg white,
½ cupful of white grape juice,
  Shaved ice,
  Ginger ale.

Select a tall, straight-sided glass — an iced tea glass will do — and fill it half full with crushed ice. Turn the ice, sugar, egg white, and grape juice into a cocktail shaker; shake well, strain into the selected glass and fill with ginger ale.

HORSE'S NECK

1 bottle of ginger ale,
1 lemon.

Peel a lemon in one continuous strip; place in a tall, straight-sided glass with one end over the edge of the glass, and add several pieces of ice. Pour over this the ginger ale. If one desires it, a few drops of bitters may be added.

HAPPY THOUGHT

1 cupful of iced tea,
1 teaspoonful of lemon juice,
3 drops of bitters,
  Ginger ale.

Put into a tall glass several pieces of ice and a cupful of cold tea; add the lemon juice and the bitters; pour in enough ginger ale to fill the glass.

MARY'S FAVORITE

1 cupful of crushed ice,
⅓ cupful of lemon juice,
⅓ cupful of orange juice,
2 teaspoonfuls of sugar,
1 slice of orange,
1 cherry,
1 spray of mint.

Mix the orange and lemon juice with the sugar and stir until the sugar is dissolved. Put a cupful of crushed ice into a tall glass and pour the fruit juice over. Add one cherry, a slice of orange and a spray of mint. Serve with a straw.

ORANGE STREAM

⅓ cupful of shaved ice,
1 egg,
2 tablespoonfuls of vanilla syrup,
2 tablespoonfuls of orange syrup,
3 drops of bitters,
⅓ teaspoonful of orange extract,
  Ice cream.

Put the shaved ice into a tall, straight-sided glass, pour over it the syrups, extract and the bitters; add a generous spoonful of ice cream, and fill the glass with carbonated water, using a syphon. Serve with a straw and a spoon.

HARVEST PUNCH

Every one who works in the fields at harvest time knows the necessity for a cooling drink, whether it be farmer or farmerette. When sending the jug to the field try this.

1 gallon of spring water,
½ cupful of sugar,
½ cupful of cider vinegar,
1 teaspoonful of ground ginger.

Mix the sugar, ginger and vinegar until the sugar is dissolved and the ginger blended; pour into the spring water and send to the field at once.

OATMEAL WATER

This is also an excellent thing for the harvesters.

1 quart of oatmeal gruel (see English oatmeal gruel),
1 gallon of spring water.

Mix the oatmeal gruel with a gallon of fresh spring water and pour it into a jug and send to the field at once.

SARSAPARILLA WITH CREAM

1 bottle sarsaparilla,
½ pint of cream,
Ice.

Put a tablespoonful of cracked ice in a tall, straight-sided glass, add two tablespoonfuls of cream, and fill the glass with sarsaparilla. This will be sufficient for two glasses the size of iced tea glasses if one uses the sarsaparilla which is put up in bottles the size of imported ginger ale bottles. There is an excellent brand of domestic make on the market.

EGG PHOSPHATE

4 tablespoonfuls of orange syrup,
1 egg,

Acid phosphate,
Ice,
Soda.

Use an iced tea glass; put a tablespoonful of cracked ice
in first, add the syrup, egg and a half teaspoonful of acid
phosphate. Fill the glass with club soda and shake well.
One may make this in a cocktail shaker or by using a shaker-
top with the glass. Sprinkle a little grated nutmeg on top
before serving.

Acid phosphate may be purchased at any drug store.

LEMON EGG PHOSPHATE

3 tablespoonfuls of lemon syrup,
1 egg,
  Acid phosphate,
  Soda,
  Ice.

Use a shaker or shaker-top on the tall glass, as one wishes.
Put a tablespoonful of cracked ice, the egg, syrup and a half
teaspoonful of acid phosphate in the glass; shake well, fill
with soda, strain into a straight, tall serving glass and
sprinkle with grated nutmeg.

GRAPE EGG PHOSPHATE

1 tablespoonful of plain syrup,
1 cupful of grape juice,
1 egg,
  Acid phosphate,
  Ice.

Put three tablespoonfuls of cracked ice, the plain syrup,
grape juice, egg and a half teaspoonful of acid phosphate
in a shaker and shake thoroughly. Strain into a tall serving
glass and serve.

LOGANBERRY EGG PHOSPHATE

3 tablespoonfuls of plain syrup,
4 tablespoonfuls of loganberry juice,
1 egg,
  Acid phosphate,
  Soda,
  Ice.

Put the plain syrup, egg, two tablespoonfuls of cracked ice, a half teaspoonful of acid phosphate, loganberry juice and enough club soda to nearly fill the glass into a shaker. Shake thoroughly, strain into a serving glass and serve.

XI — SUNDAES

Because of the popularity of sundaes, and the preference shown by many for them instead of sweet or fruit drinks, I shall give a goodly number of suggestions for making these delightful concoctions.

I shall give recipes for sauces to be used on them, as well as suggestions for preserving and drying cherries.

While the recipes given for syrups, both plain and flavored, are given primarily for the making of punches, bowls, cups and the like, there is no reason why these should not be used on sundaes, in fact there is every reason why they should.

It is also possible and most advisable to use the syrup from canned or preserved fruits on sundaes, as there is almost always more syrup in a jar of fruit than is needed, and it may be used to advantage in this way.

One may make marshmallow cream or purchase it ready for use. One candy manufacturer in New York puts out an excellent article at a very reasonable price.

While one almost invariably sees pecan nuts used for topping sundaes, it is not at all essential that they should be; walnuts, either domestic or English, may be used with equal success. If obtainable, try butternuts broken in pieces.

One may use either the short-stemmed, wide-topped sherbet glasses or the wide long-stemmed champagne glasses for service. These are equally attractive.

Select small plates, place a doylie on each and place the glass on that. Lay a small spoon on the plate.

In most instances, a rounded spoonful of ice cream is placed in the glass first, then the syrup or sauce is poured over that, and nuts, or chopped fruits, or both are then added.

One may use any flavor ice cream one desires, and because of this I have given a number of recipes for ice creams, not only for making sundaes but because they, too, quench the thirst.

There is one important thing to remember when making sundaes; they must *never* look mussy! Even though a number of different things are used in the making, it is not at all necessary to use such haste that they will not look appetizing.

After the cream is in the glass, pour the syrup or sauce over carefully, being sure not to drip it; add the next thing just as carefully as the first, and if nuts are to top the dish, add only enough to stay where they are meant to stay — *on the top*. If the nuts fall to the service plate the whole service is spoiled in appearance.

An attractive service makes for the success of the hostess.

Use vanilla ice cream as the foundation;

Plain syrup, diced bananas, nuts.

Plain syrup, marshmallow cream, chopped bananas, nuts.

Caramel sauce, diced bananas, nuts.

Caramel sauce, sliced bananas, marshmallow cream, nuts.

Caramel sauce, sliced bananas, whipped cream, nuts.

Caramel sauce, diced bananas, whipped cream, chopped cherries.

For a Banana Split use,

1 peeled banana cut in half lengthwise; lay side by side on plate, put one spoonful of vanilla ice cream on one end, strawberry ice cream on the other; cover with any fresh fruit in season, crushed and mixed with plain syrup. Sprinkle with chopped nuts, or if one wishes such a variety, add whipped cream before the nuts.

Use vanilla ice cream as the foundation;

Cherry syrup, chopped nuts,

Cherry syrup, whole cherries,

Cherry syrup, marshmallow cream, chopped cherries,

Cherry syrup, marshmallow cream, broken nuts, one Maraschino cherry.

Cherry syrup, marshmallow cream, chopped cherries,

Use with vanilla ice cream;
Hot chocolate sauce,
Hot chocolate sauce, nuts,
Chocolate sauce,
Chocolate sauce, nuts.
Chocolate sauce, marshmallow cream, nuts.
Chocolate sauce, marshmallow cream, nuts, malted milk
sprinkled over all.
Chocolate sauce, whipped cream, nuts.
Chocolate sauce, whipped cream, nuts, cherries.
Chocolate sauce, marshmallow, chopped figs.
Chocolate sauce, marshmallow, chopped dates.
Chocolate caramel sauce, nuts.
Chocolate caramel sauce, marshmallow cream, shredded
cocoanut.
Chocolate fudge sauce,
Chocolate fudge sauce, nuts.
Chocolate fudge sauce, marshmallow cream, nuts.
Chocolate fudge sauce, marshmallow cream, nuts, cherry.

Use with chocolate ice cream;
Chocolate sauce, marshmallow cream, nuts.
Marshmallow cream, nuts, chopped cherries.
Marshmallow cream, chopped raisins, chopped nuts.
Chocolate sauce, chopped raisins.

Use with vanilla ice cream;
Coffee sauce,
Coffee sauce, whipped cream, nuts.
Coffee syrup, marshmallow cream, chopped cherries.
Coffee syrup, marshmallow sauce, nuts.

With coffee ice cream;
Caramel sauce, nuts.
Caramel sauce, whipped cream, nuts.
Caramel sauce, whipped cream, cherries.

Plain syrup, marshmallow cream, cherry.
Plain syrup, marshallow cream, nuts.

With vanilla ice cream:
Maple fudge sauce.
Maple fudge sauce, nuts.
Maple fudge sauce, nuts, cherries.
Maple fudge sauce, marshmallow cream, nuts.
Hot maple sauce.
Hot maple sauce, nuts.
Berkshire maple sauce (hot) nuts.

With vanilla ice cream:
Honey sauce, whipped cream.
Honey sauce, whipped cream, nuts.
Honey sauce, chopped cherries.
Honey sauce, chopped raisins.

Use with vanilla ice cream;
Orange sauce, nuts.
Orange sauce, small sections of orange pulp, nuts.
Orange sauce, marshmallow cream, nuts.
Orange sauce, marshmallow cream, chopped cherries.
Orange sauce, marshmallow cream, shredded pineapple,
nuts.

Use with vanilla ice cream;
Prune sauce.
Prune sauce, marshmallow cream.
Prune sauce, marshmallow cream, nuts.

Use with peach ice cream;
Peaches sliced thin, whipped cream, cherries.
Marshmallow cream, peaches crushed and mixed with
plain syrup.
Crushed peaches, whipped cream, chopped nuts.
Caramel sauce, crushed peaches.
Caramel sauce, marshmallow cream, crushed peaches.
Plain syrup, crushed peaches, whipped cream.

Use with vanilla ice cream;

Place one half peach in the bottom of the glass, one spoonful of ice cream, place the second half over this and pour raspberry syrup over all.

Crushed peaches mixed with plain syrup.

Crushed peaches, marshmallow cream, nuts.

Half fresh peach over cream, cover with peach syrup, whipped cream, nuts.

Use with vanilla ice cream;

Shredded pineapple, plain syrup, whipped cream.

Shredded pineapple, pineapple syrup, nuts.

Caramel sauce, chopped pineapple.

Use with vanilla ice cream;

Caramel sauce, crushed raspberries, nuts.

Caramel sauce, crushed raspberries, whipped cream, whole preserved raspberries.

Caramel sauce, raspberries, whipped cream.

Caramel sauce, preserved peaches, sliced, crushed raspberries.

Use with strawberry ice cream;

Crushed strawberries.

Crushed strawberries, whipped cream.

Crushed strawberries, marshmallow cream, whole strawberries.

Use with vanilla ice cream;

Crushed strawberries.

Crushed strawberries, plain syrup.

Crushed strawberries, whipped cream, nuts.

Preserved strawberries,

Preserved strawberries, whipped cream.

Preserved strawberries, marshmallow cream, selected strawberries.

Preserved strawberries, whipped cream, a cherry.

With vanilla ice cream;
Crushed raspberries, plain syrup.
Crushed raspberries, whipped cream.
Crushed raspberries, whipped cream, chopped cherries.
Preserved raspberries, chopped nuts.
Preserved raspberries, marshmallow cream.
Preserved raspberries, marshmallow cream, chopped cherries.

Use with pistachio ice cream;
Caramel sauce, chopped cherries, nuts.
Marshmallow cream, chopped cherries, pistachio nuts finely chopped.
Chocolate sauce, nuts.
Chocolate sauce, marshmallow cream, pistachio nuts.

With vanilla ice cream;
Rose sauce, marshmallow cream, candied rose leaves.
Rose sauce, whipped cream, candied rose leaves, nuts.

With vanilla ice cream;
Caramel sauce, whipped cream, candied violets.
Plain syrup, whipped cream, candied violets.

With vanilla ice cream;
Tutti frutti sauce.
Tutti frutti sauce, whipped cream, nuts.
Fruit sauce.
Fruit sauce, whipped cream.
Fruit sauce, whipped cream, nuts.

Chocolate ice cream;
Tutti frutti sauce.
Rose sauce.
Rose sauce, whipped cream.

With vanilla ice cream;
Raspberry sauce.

Raspberry sauce, marshmallow cream.

Raspberry sauce, marshmallow cream, nuts, chopped cherries.

XII — SAUCES FOR SUNDAES

Because it would seem folly to give suggestions for sundaes without recipes for making the sauces to be served on them, I am giving several.

While these sauces are given here to use on sundaes, there is no good reason why they may not be used for puddings and desserts.

HEAVY FUDGE SAUCE

2 cupfuls of sugar,
2 squares of chocolate,
1 cupful of milk,
1¼ tablespoonfuls of butter,
½ teaspoonful of vanilla.

Melt the chocolate, putting it into a double boiler; add the milk and cook directly over the fire until it is well blended; add the sugar and cook slowly until smooth. Keep hot in the double boiler or in a chafing dish until ready to serve.

This should be the consistency to pour readily.

MARSHMALLOW SAUCE

¾ cupful of sugar,
¼ cupful of milk,
½ pound of marshmallows,
2 tablespoonfuls of water.

Boil the sugar and milk in a double boiler for about six or seven minutes, until it spins a thread. Allow this to become luke warm, then beat until thick and white. Put the double boiler back on the fire and stir until thin enough to pour. Melt the marshmallows and water, pour the syrup

142

over them, beating constantly. Keep warm until ready to
serve.

MARSHMALLOW SAUCE NO. 2

½ pound of marshmallows,
1 cupful of sugar,
⅓ cupful of boiling water,
1 egg white,
¾ cupful of Maraschino cherries.

Into the upper part of the double boiler turn half a pound
of marshmallows and melt them slowly until they will pour
readily. Dissolve one cupful of sugar in one-third of a cupful of boiling water and cook without stirring (after it
begins to bubble hard) for eight minutes. Pour gently on
to the stiffly whipped white of one egg and beat steadily until
thick and creamy. Add the marshmallow syrup and a small
cupful of drained and chopped Maraschino cherries.

MARSHMALLOW SAUCE WITH SYRUP

½ pound of marshmallows,
1 cupful of corn syrup,
¼ cupful of hot water,
1 egg white,
  Chopped cherries.

Melt the marshmallows in a double boiler. Boil the syrup
and water together until bubbling hot, then pour slowly on
the stiffly beaten white of the egg. Beat until creamy and
thick, then add the marshmallows. Chop a tablespoonful
of candied Maraschino cherries and add to the sauce.

MAPLE FUDGE SAUCE

1 pound of maple sugar,
1½ pints of rich milk,
1 tablespoonful of butter,
  A pinch of soda.

Cook the maple sugar (which should have been grated), milk and soda until it boils; continue to boil for five minutes, stir in the butter and keep hot over boiling water. A double boiler or a chafing dish would be the best means of doing so.

HOT MAPLE SAUCE

1 cupful of thick maple syrup,
⅓ cupful of cream,
Chopped nuts.

Butter the inside of a granite saucepan and add a cupful of thick maple syrup and one-third of a cupful of cream. Then boil until the syrup forms a soft ball when tested in cold water. Pour while hot, over each portion of cream and sprinkle thickly with chopped nut meats.

BERKSHIRE HOT MAPLE SAUCE

1 cupful of maple syrup,
1 tablespoonful of butter,
⅓ cupful of top milk.

Put the butter in a saucepan and when melted stir in the maple syrup. Then when hot add the top milk slowly; boil until it begins to thicken slightly, then cool partially and serve.

PRUNE SAUCE

1 cupful of well cooked prunes,
4 or 5 candied green-gage plums,
6 candied cherries,
1 orange,
1 tablespoonful of lemon juice,
⅓ cupful of sugar,
½ cupful of chopped nut meats.

Cut the prunes in small pieces; peel the orange, separate into sections and remove the membrane; then cut into pieces; chop the plums and cherries and mix the fruit. Add lemon juice and sugar, stir and allow to stand for a half hour. Place a generous spoonful on each serving of cream; top with a spoonful of nuts.

HONEY SAUCE

2 tablespoonfuls of butter,
1 tablespoonful of cornstarch,
¼ cupful of honey,
½ cupful of hot water.

Melt the butter and blend with the cornstarch. Add honey and hot water. Cook until it thickens and serve hot.

COFFEE SAUCE WITH SYRUP

1 cupful of strong coffee,
1 cupful of corn syrup,
2 egg yolks,
1 cupful of cream, sweetened.

Heat the coffee until the boiling point is reached; add the egg yolks beaten light, then the syrup; cook until it begins to thicken but do not allow it to boil. Take from the fire, add the cream, whipped stiff, and a few drops of vanilla.

COFFEE SAUCE WITH SUGAR

2 eggs,
¼ cupful of sugar,
1 cupful of strong coffee,
1 cupful of whipped cream,
  Sugar (powdered.)

Beat the yolks of the eggs with one-fourth cupful of sugar. Add one cupful of strong coffee (strained) and cook slowly over hot water, stirring constantly until well thickened. Do not boil. Remove from the fire and, when cold, mix 1 cupful of sweetened whipped cream which has been flavored with a few drops of vanilla extract.

CHOCOLATE SAUCE WITH SYRUP

  1 cupful of syrup,
  1½ squares of chocolate,
  ⅓ cupful of water,
  ¼ teaspoonful of vanilla.

Melt the chocolate and pour on gradually the hot syrup, prepared by adding water to corn syrup and boiling for three minutes. Cool slightly and flavor with vanilla.

CHOCOLATE CARAMEL SAUCE

  2 ounces of unsweetened chocolate,
  2 cupfuls of dark brown sugar,
  1 tablespoonful of butter,
  ⅔ cupful of rich top milk or cream,
  ¼ teaspoonful of vanilla extract.

If an agate boiler is used, and a very little butter heated in it, and allowed to run over the surface used, the sauce will not stick to the pan.

Shave the chocolate and melt in the buttered upper part of the double boiler, and add the sugar gradually; mix well, and add the butter; cook until well blended and pour in the top milk or cream slowly. Cook over a very low fire until it forms a soft ball if tried in cold water. Take from the fire, add the vanilla, and use over vanilla ice cream.

If it is not to be used at once keep it hot in the double boiler.

FRUIT SAUCE

  ⅓ cupful of dates,
  ½ cupful of Maraschino cherries,
  ½ cupful of figs,
  ⅓ cupful of chopped almonds,
  ½ cupful of honey,
  ½ cupful of syrup from the cherries.

Remove the pits from the dates and cut into small pieces,

chop the cherries, cut the figs into small pieces and chop
(or break into pieces) the nuts. Mix, and pour the syrup
of the cherries and the honey over the mixture, allowing to
stand until thoroughly blended. Keep near the ice if
possible.

STRAWBERRY SAUCE

1 quart of berries,
1 cupful of powdered sugar.

Wash and hull the berries, mash with a silver fork, add
the sugar, stir well, and allow to stand for two hours in a
cold place.

ORANGE SAUCE

3 oranges,
2 egg whites,
1 cupful of powdered sugar.

Grate the rind of half an orange and add to it the juice
of three oranges. Whip the whites of the eggs until dry
and stiff, add the sugar and then the orange juice.

This, heaped on ice cream, is as delightful as it is unusual.

TUTTI FRUTTI SAUCE

$\frac{1}{2}$ cupful of chopped candied cherries,
$\frac{1}{2}$ cupful of chopped seeded raisins,
$\frac{1}{2}$ cupful of chopped figs,
$\frac{1}{2}$ cupful of dates,
   Mix with maple syrup.

Chop the different fruits and mix enough maple syrup to
blend but not enough to make a great deal of liquid.

CANNED, PRESERVED AND DRIED CHERRIES

(For use in making sundaes)

There may be several reasons why one prefers to use home-canned or dried cherries instead of using those commercially prepared. To can them at home, the first thing to remember is; the fruit should be well ripened and the cherries will be far better if it is possible to obtain them directly from the trees. If one is fortunate enough to be able to get them from the trees, see that they hang at least four days after they are considered ripe, for they will be larger, riper and sweeter.

Another thing to bear in mind, is that cherries should be simmered and never boiled.

It is quite possible to use any canned cherries one may have, or may purchase, in making sundaes, or those put up commercially for this purpose alone.

CANNED CHERRIES

The amount of fruit depends upon the desire of the hotesss, for she may have a few she wishes to can, or a great many; the process is the same.

Cherries,
2 cupfuls of water,
1 cupful of sugar.

Wash and pit the cherries, put them in sterilized jars, adjust the rubbers (new ones), and pour over the boiling syrup, made of the sugar and water boiled. Pour in enough syrup to nearly overflow. Partially seal the jar and place in a sterilizer, either commercial or home-made, and nearly cover with boiling water. It has been found satisfactory by the writer to allow the water to reach just *below* the top. Sterilize for sixteen minutes.

CANNED CHERRIES WITHOUT SYRUP

If one cares to can the cherries without using syrup, pour plain boiling water over the cherries in the jars, in place of the syrup and sterilize for a half hour. After sterilization, complete the seal, invert to test for leakage, allow to cool, wrap in dark paper and store.

PRESERVED CHERRIES

Remove the pits from the largest cherries obtainable; allow a pound of sugar and one cupful of water to each pound of fruit. Melt the sugar in the water, let it come to a boil and skim thoroughly. Then add the cherries and allow them to simmer for twenty minutes. Take out with a skimmer, pack into sterilized hot jars and boil down the syrup until quite thick. Fill the jars to overflowing and seal air-tight, using new rubbers and hot covers.

PRESERVES AND SHRUB FROM THE SAME CHERRIES

Stone the cherries and cover with vinegar. Stand in a cool place for twenty-four hours and drain off the fruit juice and the vinegar. To each pint of juice add a scant pound of sugar, simmer for twenty-five minutes and bottle air-tight. Put the drained cherries in a stone crock with alternate layers of granulated sugar, allowing three-quarters of a pound of sugar for each pint of fruit. Keep the crock covered and in a cool place. Every eighteen hours stir the fruit and sugar carefully for a period of eight days. The uncooked preserves can be put in small jars and paraffined, but they need not be sealed air-tight.

MOCK MARASCHINO CHERRIES

Select the largest sized cherries one can find and remove the pits, saving all the juice. Measure fruit and juice and allow an equal amount of sugar. Drain the cherries and set on the ice. Put the juice and sugar into a preserving kettle, cook to a thick syrup and add the cherries. Simmer for fifteen minutes. Drain off half the cherry syrup, add an equal amount of white grape juice, bring quickly to the boil and seal as for preserved fruit.

DRIED CHERRIES

The larger the cherry the more satisfactory if dried to use for sundaes.

Wash, stem and pit the cherries; spread in thin layers on a drying tray. (Commercial driers are inexpensive and very satisfactory.) Dry from two to four hours, starting at 110 degrees F. Condition them by placing in composition or paper boxes and pouring them from box to box every day for four days. This is to insure even drying. If too moist, return to the drier for a short time, and again pour into the boxes, and again "condition" them.

XIII — ICE CREAMS, SORBETS, SHER-BETS, WATER ICES AND GRANITS

Giving recipes for ice creams and the like in a book given to telling of beverages would seem a queer conceit, were it not for the fact that ice creams, sherbets and water ices are often used to quench the thirst; this is my reason and my only excuse, should an excuse be needed.

VANILLA ICE CREAM

1 quart of cream,
¾ cupful of honey,
1 cupful of milk,
1 tablespoonful of vanilla extract.

Heat the milk, add the honey, and stir until melted and thoroughly mixed. Allow to cool somewhat; add the cream, vanilla and a pinch of salt (a very small pinch), and freeze.

VANILLA ICE CREAM (French)

2 cupfuls of scalded milk,
1 cupful of sugar,
3 eggs,
⅛ teaspoonful of salt,
1 quart of thin cream,
2 tablespoonfuls of vanilla.

Make a custard of the first four ingredients. Strain and cool the custard and add to it the cream and vanilla. Freeze until firm, then pack in ice and salt.

INEXPENSIVE ICE CREAM

1¼ cupfuls of sugar,
1 quart of milk,
2 tablespoonfuls of cornstarch,
3 eggs,
Desired extract and a pinch of salt.

Heat the milk, add the syrup and the cornstarch, which should have been moistened with a little cold milk; cook until it begins to thicken, add a pinch of salt and the beaten eggs. Boil, strain, cool and freeze.

With this as a foundation one may add any flavoring desired, or any crushed fruit. Coffee or chocolate may also be used. Very strong coffee is needed, but the amount of milk should be reduced in proportion.

PISTACHIO ICE CREAM

2 cupfuls of scalded milk,
1 tablespoonful of flour,
1 cupful of sugar,
1 egg,
⅛ teaspoonful of salt,
1 quart thin cream,
1 tablespoonful of vanilla extract,
1 teaspoonful of almond extract.

Mix flour, sugar and milk, add egg, slightly beaten, and milk gradually. Cook until it has the consistency of a soft custard. Let this custard cool and add cream and flavoring, color with leaf green; strain and freeze.

ORANGE ICE CREAM

2 cupfuls of sugar,
1 cupful of water,
2 cupfuls of orange juice,
¼ cupful of candied orange peel,
1 cupful of cream,

2 egg yolks,
1 cupful of double cream.

Boil the water and sugar eight minutes. Add the orange juice. Make a custard of the cream and egg yolks. Cool and add to the first mixture with the heavy cream beaten stiff. Freeze. When nearly frozen add the orange peel. The dish is given a " different " look if it is served with candied orange peel.

MARSHMALLOW ICE CREAM

1½ cupfuls of milk,
½ cupful of heavy cream,
¾ cupful of sugar,
1 junket tablet,
1 tablespoonful cold water,
2 heaping tablespoonfuls of marshmallow cream,
1 tablespoonful of vanilla.

Put milk, cream and sugar into the can of freezer. Set in hot water until luke warm, add junket tablet dissolved in cold water, and allow to stand until firm. Add vanilla and marshmallow cream, mix thoroughly and freeze, using three parts ice to one part salt.

FROZEN PUDDING

1 pint of milk,
1 cupful of sugar,
3 eggs,
1 teaspoonful of cornstarch,
⅛ teaspoonful of salt,
1 pint thin cream,
½ teaspoonful of vanilla,
1 cupful of diced marshmallows,
1 cupful of thinly sliced peaches,
1 cupful of shredded pineapple,
1 cupful crystallized cherries.

Beat the yolks of the eggs until very light, add sugar, cornstarch and salt. Beat into this the scalded milk, place in a double boiler and cook until it will coat the spoon. Remove from the fire and when cold add the cream, vanilla and stiffly beaten whites of the eggs. Pour into a freezer, add the marshmallows and fruit and freeze until firm, then pack and allow to stand for several hours.

COCOANUT ICE CREAM

4 cupfuls of milk,
2½ tablespoonfuls of cornstarch,
 2 eggs,
 ¾ cupfuls of honey,
 1 teaspoonful of vanilla extract,
 1 cupful of chopped fresh cocoanut or shredded cocoanut,
   Preserved cherries,
   Milk or water.

Heat the milk in a double boiler. Blend the cornstarch with a little milk or water and add to the hot milk and stir until it begins to thicken. Add the beaten eggs and honey, cook for a minute or two; add vanilla and cocoanut. Freeze, serve in attractive tall stemmed goblets; top with cocoanut and cherries.

ROSE ICE CREAM (with condensed milk)

 2 cans of condensed milk,
3½ cupfuls of water,
 2 teaspoonfuls of rose extract,
 3 tablespoonfuls of cornstarch,
 ¼ cupful of milk, or water,
 1 teaspoonful of vanilla,
 1 teaspoonful of orange extract,
   Red vegetable coloring.

Mix one can of condensed milk with two cupfuls of water; add the rose extract and enough red vegetable coloring to make the color desired. Strain and freeze.

Boil the remaining water (1½ cupfuls) and stir in the other can of condensed milk. Moisten the cornstarch with a little milk or water, blend with the milk and water, stirring constantly for five or six minutes. Allow to cool, add flavoring, strain and freeze. Place these creams in separate layers in a wet mold, place the cover on securely, pack and freeze. This should stand at least two hours.

PINEAPPLE ICE CREAM

1½ cupfuls of hot milk,
2 eggs,
½ cupful of honey,
2 cupfuls of shredded pineapple.
1 cupful of cream,

Beat the eggs, mix with the milk and honey; cook until smooth, stirring constantly. Allow to cool, add cream and freeze. When serving this cream, a generous spoonful of sweetened whipped cream is a delightful addition.

STRAWBERRY ICE CREAM

This is not difficult to make and approaches the flavor of the fresh fruit more nearly than most creams in which fresh strawberries are used.

½ pint of thick cream,
1 pint of milk,
2 tablespoonfuls of cornstarch,
2 eggs,
3 tablespoonfuls of sugar,
½ teaspoonful of vanilla,
1 cupful of strawberry jam,
    Small pinch of salt.

Make a boiled custard of the milk, cornstarch, salt and the beaten eggs. Add the vanilla, cool and fold in a half pint of cream which has been whipped until stiff. Put in freezer and freeze slowly for five or six minutes; open the freezer and stir in a full cupful of strawberry jam. Re-cover and continue to freeze until firm.

GREEN TEA ICE CREAM

1 pint of milk,
1 tablespoonful of green tea,
1 pint of cream,
¾ cupful of sugar,
3 eggs,
½ teaspoonful of vanilla.

Pour one pint of boiling milk over one tablespoonful of green tea, and allow to stand on the back of the range or on an asbestos mat over a low gas flame for five minutes; strain through a double thickness of fine cheesecloth. To this add the cream, beaten eggs, sugar and vanilla, and stir until it thickens. Add a little green vegetable color. Place in a cold dish and allow to cool. Freeze, repack, and allow to stand until ready for use.

EASY PEACH ICE CREAM

1 pint of peach pulp and the juice,
1 cupful of sugar,
1 quart of cream.

Crush the peaches, using enough to make a pint of pulp. Save all the juice. Add the sugar to the juice and pulp; then add the cream, whipped as stiff as possible. Blend and freeze.

SOME UNUSUAL FROZEN DAINTIES

COFFEE PARFAIT

1 pint of thick cream,
1½ cupfuls of confectioner's sugar,
½ cupful of strong coffee,

½ teaspoonful of vanilla,
½ teaspoonful of gelatine,
  Milk.

Dissolve the gelatine in two tablespoonfuls of milk, and pour the hot coffee over, stirring well; add sugar and vanilla. Fold in the cream, whipped stiff, pour into the freezer, pack in ice and salt and allow to stand for at least four hours.

Serve in attractive tall glasses, topped with a generous spoonful of sweetened whipped cream.

APRICOT PARFAIT

1½ cupfuls of crushed apricots (canned or fresh),
 2 tablespoonfuls of lemon juice,
 ¾ cupful of sugar,
 1 teaspoonful of gelatine,
 2 eggs,
 1 cupful of thick cream.

Mash the fruit and press through a fine sieve, add the lemon juice and sugar and heat until it reaches the boiling point, stirring constantly; beat the yolks of the eggs until very light and add slowly to the fruit mixture while hot; return to the fire and cook until a custard-like consistency. Dissolve the gelatine in a very little water and add to the fruit and eggs; allow to cool; chill; beat the whites of the eggs until stiff, and the cream until firm, and add both to the fruit mixture.

Pour into a mold, pack in ice and salt and allow to stand for several hours; serve in tall narrow glasses.

CHERRY PARFAIT

 1 cupful of thick cream,
 ¾ cupful of sugar,
 ½ cupful of water,
 2 egg whites,
 1 tablespoonful of gelatine,

½ cupful of marshmallows,
1¼ cupfuls of stoned cherries (canned red cherries may be used),
1 cupful of cherry juice,
2 tablespoonfuls of lemon juice.

Cut the marshmallows into very small pieces, and cut the cherries in halves; combine these with the cherry juice and allow to stand for two hours.

Boil the sugar and water until it will "spin a thread" and pour slowly over the stiffly beaten whites of the eggs, beating constantly. Allow it to become chilled, and stir in the stiffly whipped cream. Soak the gelatine in a little water and melt over hot water. Strain into the fruit mixture, beating briskly, until well blended; allow this to cool and when it begins to thicken, beat in the whipped cream. Pour into a wet mold, pack in ice, and salt, and allow to stand for three hours or more. Serve in parfait glasses, topped with whipped cream and a cherry.

GRAPE AND PINEAPPLE PARFAIT

2 cupfuls of milk,
2 egg whites,
1 cupful of sugar,
½ cupful of chopped nut meats,
¼ teaspoonful of powdered nutmeg,
4 cupfuls of pineapple juice,
  Preserved grapes,
  Whipped cream,
  Rose extract,
  Crystallized mint.

The foundation of this delightful parfait is made in the following manner: Scald the two cupfuls of milk and add the beaten egg whites; stir in the sugar and chopped nuts. Cook until thick, add the nutmeg; cool and add the pineapple juice and freeze.

Put a spoonful of frozen mixture in the bottom of a tall glass, then a spoonful of preserved grapes, and fill the glass with the cream. Top with whipped cream which has been sweetened and flavored with rose. A crystallized mint adds to the attractiveness of this unusual parfait.

RASPBERRY PARFAIT

1 pint of cream,
1 pint of raspberries,
  Sugar.

Whip a pint of cream until very stiff, and sweeten with powdered sugar slightly. Cook the raspberries until broken, which should not take more than five or six minutes; press out all the juice and pulp possible, and reboil with three-fourths as much sugar as juice. Allow this to cool. Spread whipped cream in a mold, and pour some of the raspberry syrup over, and add more cream, and so fill the mold. Unless one prefers, then the syrup and whipped cream may be lightly mixed before packing in the mold. Pack in ice and salt and allow to stand for several hours

MAPLE BISQUE

2 eggs,
½ pint of cream,
½ cupful of maple syrup,
  Vanilla.

Beat the yolks of the eggs until very light, add the maple syrup slowly, and heat over a slow fire, stirring constantly until it reaches the boiling point. Boil for one minute only; remove from the fire, strain and cool.

Beat the cream until firm and add to the stiffly beaten whites of the eggs. Pour the syrup mixture over this slowly, beating constantly; add the vanilla. Pour into a mold, pack and freeze.

PEACH MELBA

1 pint of heavy cream,
1 pint of milk,
1 cupful of sugar,
1 tablespoonful of gelatine,
½ teaspoonful of vanilla,
1 can of large peaches or ½ dozen selected peaches.

Heat the milk and sugar, until the sugar is thoroughly dissolved; dissolve gelatine in a little cold milk and add to the heated milk and sugar.

Allow this to cool, add the cream whipped stiffly, flavor and pour into the freezer. Freeze until the crank turns very hard; remove the dasher, repack and allow to stand for two hours.

When ready to serve, place a half peach on the bottom of a long stemmed glass, fill with the cream, put the other half of the peach on top and top with raspberry syrup, then the whipped cream.

SAUCE.— To one cupful of raspberry jam add one cupful of boiling water sweetened a bit; boil for five minutes, strain, chill and use.

PEACH DELIGHT

2 cupfuls of water,
¾ cupful of honey,
1 teaspoonful of gelatine,
1 cupful of peach pulp,
1 lemon,
1 orange,
1 cupful of cream, whipped.

Bring the water and honey to the boiling point and continue to cook for twenty minutes. Add the gelatine which should have been soaked and dissolved in a little cold water; strain and allow to cool.

When cold add the peach pulp, orange pulp, orange juice

and the juice of half a lemon. Turn into a freezer and freeze slowly. Serve in attractive glasses, topped with whipped cream.

FROZEN PEACHES

4 cupfuls of mashed peaches,
1½ cupfuls of sugar,
1 teaspoonful of lemon juice.

Wipe the peaches with a damp cloth; pare and put the skins and one peach pit in two cupfuls of cold water and allow to boil for twenty minutes; strain through a sieve, pressing out all the juice; add the sugar, boil until the sugar is thoroughly dissolved and set aside to cool.

When cold add the mashed peaches and the lemon juice and freeze.

If one wishes, a spoonful of whipped cream added to each serving adds perceptibly to this dainty.

CRUSHED PEACHES

Peaches,
Sugar,
Cream.

The housekeeper often finds that peaches are too ripe to slice and use with cream; in which case it is wise and economical to skin them, remove the stones and mash through a coarse sieve, adding sugar, honey or syrup to taste. If the peaches are the kind which have little flavor, a little lemon juice is desirable. Serve in low stemmed sherbet glasses, topped with whipped cream, on which a candied cherry may be placed.

FROSTED BANANA CREAM

Bananas,
Sugar,
Lemon juice.

Select only very ripe bananas; mash to a paste, sweeten with powdered sugar and flavor with a few drops of lemon juice. Press through a sieve and to each cupful of banana add a half cupful of whipped cream. Mix and serve in attractive glasses, and sprinkle with powdered sugar.

SORBETS, SHERBETS, ICES, GRANITS

The difference in sorbets, sherbets, ices and granits is slight, still each fills its own particular purpose and place. Sorbets are supposed to be served after the meat course, and while the same ingredients are used they are not frozen as long or as smooth as sherbets. Sherbets are smoother and firmer, and may well take the place of ice cream as a dessert. Water ices are made the same as sherbets, leaving out the egg whites. Granits are water ices frozen slightly; in fact so they will pour, and may be used as a drink.

BLACKBERRY SORBET

2 cupfuls of sugar syrup,
3 tablespoonfuls of lemon juice,
1 cupful of rich milk,
2 quarts of blackberries,
1 tablespoonful of gelatine,
2 egg whites.

Press the berries through a sieve fine enough to keep the seeds from passing through, but pass the pulp through. Add the syrup and lemon juice. Dissolve the gelatine in a little water, and add to the berry juice and milk. Pour this mixture into the freezer and turn until it begins to thicken. Add the stiffly beaten whites of the eggs and continue to freeze until fluffy, but not so smooth as for sherbet. This is a fine distinction, but still it is considered worth differentiation.

When this " fluffy " stage is reached remove the dasher, repack and allow to stand for about two hours.

PLUM SHERBET

While any of these recipes may be made into either sherbet or sorbet, I will give from now on only the sherbet recipes.

   1 quart of ripe plums (preferably red)
   2 cupfuls of sugar syrup,
   2 egg whites.

Select only very ripe plums; wash, remove pits, and press through a sieve. There should be a pint of this pulp and juice. Add syrup, freeze until well thickened, add the stiffly beaten whites of the eggs, and continue to turn until frozen smooth and as hard as this sort of thing can well be frozen.

CRANBERRY SHERBET

   1 quart of cranberries,
   1 quart of water,
   1 tablespoonful of gelatine,
   1½ cupfuls of syrup,
   1 egg white.

Cook the cranberries in water for ten minutes. Press through a fine sieve, return to the saucepan and add the syrup, cook for five minutes, turn into the freezer, and when partly frozen, stir in the stiffly beaten white of an egg (use two egg whites if eggs are plentiful), and finish freezing.

GRAPEFRUIT SHERBET

   2 cupfuls of water,
   2 cupfuls of grapefruit juice,
   1½ cupfuls of sugar,
   1 teaspoonful of gelatine,
   ½ cupful of white grape juice,
   1 egg white,
   2 tablespoonfuls of chopped cherries.

Boil the water and sugar together for ten minutes; soften the gelatine with a little water and stir into this syrup.

Cool, add the juice of grapefruit and the grape juice. Turn into a cold freezer and when the mixture begins to thicken well, add the stiffly beaten white of an egg and the cherries (two egg whites are better if eggs are not too expensive). Cover and freeze until firm and smooth.

GRAPE SHERBET

1 teaspoonful of gelatine,
¾ cupfuls of grape juice,
1 cupful of syrup or sugar,
½ cupful of honey,
2 tablespoonfuls of lemon juice,
½ cupful of water,
1 egg white.

Soak the gelatine in a little cold water; boil the syrup, honey and half cupful of water, and add the dissolved gelatine. Allow this to cool, add grape juice and the lemon juice and freeze. Open the freezer when slightly hard and add the stiffly beaten egg white. Re-cover and freeze until smooth and hard. (Two egg whites are better if plentiful.)

CRÉOLE LEMON SHERBET

3 lemons,
1 cupful of sugar,
2 cupfuls of water,
1 egg white.

Boil the water and sugar, and add the grated rind of one lemon. Cool, add the juice of three lemons, strain through a fine cloth, and freeze until partly frozen, remove the cover, add the egg white stiffly beaten. Cover again and freeze until smooth.

MILK SHERBET

2 lemons,
1 cupful of syrup,
3 cupfuls of whole milk,
  Candied cherries.

Mix the juice of the lemons and the syrup, add the milk very slowly, stirring constantly, as it will curdle if poured too fast. That will not spoil the sherbet, but it does not look so well and one's appetite is helped by the appearance of one's food.

Freeze the mixture, serve in attractive glasses, with a few chopped candied cherries.

ORANGE SHERBET

1 egg white,
2 cupfuls of orange juice,
2 tablespoonfuls of lemon juice,
1 cupful of water,

¾ cupfuls of sugar (brown sugar or syrup may be used).

Put the sugar in a saucepan with the water, bring to the boiling point, then cool. Add the orange and lemon juice, a pinch of salt and freeze.

Before the freezing is complete, add the egg white beaten stiffly; repack and continue to freeze until smooth.

STRAWBERRY SHERBET

1 quart of strawberries,
2 cupfuls of water,
1 tablespoonful of lemon juice,
¾ cupfuls of syrup or sugar,
1 egg white.

Wash and hull the strawberries, mash well and press through a cheesecloth. Add the syrup, lemon juice and water. Mix well, freeze partially, add the stiffly beaten egg white, and finish freezing.

RASPBERRY SHERBET

1 quart of raspberries,
1 egg white,
3 cupfuls of water,
1 cupful of syrup or sugar,

2 tablespoonfuls of lemon juice,
2 cupfuls of raspberry juice.

Mash the berries and press through a cheesecloth; pour boiling water over the the syrup; add the berry juice and lemon juice and freeze. When partially frozen, add the stiffly beaten egg white, stir in well, and continue to freeze until smooth.

EMERGENCY PEACH SHERBET

This might also be called an economical sherbet, for one may use just as many peaches as one has. For in this recipe one is supposed to use peaches too ripe for slicing.

Mash the peaches, and press through a coarse sieve and sweeten to taste. Half fill sherbet glasses with finely shaved ice and pour the sweetened peach pulp over. Top each serving with a preserved or candied cherry.

PINEAPPLE SHERBET

1½ pints of grated pineapple,
1½ cupfuls of syrup,
1 tablespoonful of gelatine,
1 pint of rich milk,
2 egg whites.

To the grated pineapple (canned may be used if fresh pineapple is not in season) add the syrup and the gelatine which has been dissolved in a small amount of water. Stir, pour into the chilled freezer, and freeze until about half frozen; open the freezer and add the milk; again turning the freezer until it turns with difficulty. Uncover, add the stiffly beaten whites of the eggs, turn until well mixed, and thoroughly hard.

If the dasher is removed and the sherbet repacked and allowed to stand to " ripen " for two hours, there will be a decided improvement in flavor and texture.

TEA SHERBET

2 cupfuls of tea,
1 cupful of sugar,
1 lemon,
1 orange,
½ cupful of water.

Melt the sugar in the water and allow to begin to boil; take from the fire and add the juice of the lemon and orange; stir well, add the tea and freeze.

APPLE ICE

1 quart of tart red apples,
1½ cupfuls of maple sugar,
3 cupfuls of water,
1 tablespoonful of lemon juice.

Wash, quarter and remove the core, but do not pare the apples. Put them into a saucepan with the water; boil rapidly until soft. Mash and add the maple sugar. When cold press through a fine sieve, add the lemon juice and freeze.

LEMON ICE

1 cupful of sugar,
3 lemons,
  Water.

Add a cupful of sugar to the zest of one lemon and the juice of three; add enough water to make a quart. Allow this to come to the boiling point, cool, strain and freeze.

LOGANBERRY ICE

2 cupfuls of loganberry juice,
1 cupful of sugar,
1 tablespoonful of lemon juice.

Boil the water; add the sugar and when cold add the lemon

and loganberry juices. Freeze until smooth and hard. Repack and allow to stand for two hours.

STRAWBERRY ICE

1 cupful of sugar,
1 cupful of water,
1 quart of strawberries.

Boil the sugar and water until it bubbles. Wash and hull the strawberries; mash and press through a cheesecloth. When the syrup is cold, add the strawberry juice and pulp; mix well and freeze.

WATERMELON ICE

Ripe melon,
1½ cupfuls of sugar,
2 oranges,
1 lemon,
½ cupful of white grape juice,
Pink vegetable coloring.

Remove the pulp from a ripe melon; press it through a fine sieve and add the sugar, lemon juice, orange juice and the zest of one orange and the grape juice. Color with enough vegetable color to make it a real watermelon pink; pack and freeze.

FRUIT GRANITS

Granits are really "snow waters," frozen only enough to admit being poured. The granits are frozen in a freezer, although the Créoles usually freeze them in the "old fashioned water jugs."

ORANGE GRANIT

1½ cupfuls of orange juice,
½ pound of sugar,
1 pint of water.

Peel six oranges very carefully, removing all the inner white part of the skin, and slice very thin. Place this in a deep bowl and sprinkle granulated sugar, allowing it to stand for five hours. Squeeze the juice from six oranges, and press the juice from the sliced ones, straining it and mixing the plain juice with this syrup. Add the water, strain and pour into a freezer; and freeze until like mush. Serve in small punch glasses.

LEMON GRANIT

1 pint of water,
½ pound of sugar,
1 cupful of lemon juice.

Extract the juice from the lemons, add the sugar and stir until dissolved; add the water and freeze until mush-like and serve in attractive punch glasses.

STRAWBERRY GRANIT

1 quart of strawberries,
1 tablespoonful of strawberry extract,
1 tablespoonful of lemon juice,
1 pound of sugar,
1½ pints of water.

Crush the berries and cover with the sugar, allowing this to stand for five hours. Strain and press through a sieve, pressing out all the juice possible. Add the lemon juice, water and the extract. Turn this into a freezer and freeze until like mush. Serve in punch glasses.

RASPBERRY GRANIT

1 quart of raspberries,
1 tablespoonful of raspberry extract,
1 pound of sugar,
½ cupful of currants,
1 pint of water.

Crush the currants and raspberries and cover with the sugar, allowing this to stand for five hours. Press through a sieve, being sure to leave no juice which can possibly be pressed out. Add the extract and water and freeze until like mush. Serve in punch glasses.

THE END.

INDEX

Classic Cocktail Resource Guide

Some ingredients found in vintage cocktail guides are unavailable or hard to come by today. However, the creation of historically accurate cocktails is a growing hobby and with a bit of Internet research, you will find recipes for bitters and syrups online, as well as manufacturers that are developing new product lines for the classic cocktail enthusiast.

Vendors

A short selection of online vendors selling bitters, mixers, syrups, wine, liqueurs, and spirits. This list is by no means complete but is a good place to start your search.

BevMo!
www.bevmo.com

Binny's Beverage Depot
www.binnys.com

The Bitter Truth
www.the-bitter-truth.com

Cocktail Kingdom
www.cocktailkingdom.com

Fee Brothers
www.feebrothers.com

Hi-Time Wine Cellars
www.hitimewine.net

Internet Wines and Spirits
www.internetwines.com

The Jug Shop
www.thejugshop.com

Monin Gourmet Flavorings
www.moninstore.com

Trader Tiki's Hand-Crafted Exotic Syrups
www.tradertiki.com

The Whiskey Exchange
www.thewhiskyexchange.com

General Interest

These sites provide background information on individual ingredients, suggestions for substitutes, current commercial availability, and recipes.

The Chanticleer Society
A Worldwide Organization of Cocktail Enthusiasts
www.chanticleersociety.org

Drink Boy
Adventures in Cocktails
www.drinkboy.com

The Internet Cocktail Database Ingredients Search
www.cocktaildb.com/ingr_search

Museum of the American Cocktail
www.museumoftheamericancocktail.org

WebTender Wiki
www.wiki.webtender.com

Classic Cocktail Guides
and Retro Bartender Books

Stuart's Fancy Drinks and How to Mix Them

Containing Clear and Practical Directions for
Mixing All Kinds of Cocktails, Sours, Egg Nog,
Sherry Cobblers, Coolers, Absinthe, Crustas,
Fizzes, Flips, Juleps, Fixes, Punches, Lemonades,
Pousse Cafes, Invalids' Drinks, Etc. Etc.

Thomas Stuart

ISBN: 978-1-880954-34-8

Classic Cocktail Guides
and Retro Bartender Books

Jack's Manual of Recipes for Fancy Mixed Drinks and How to Serve Them

A Pre-Prohibition Cocktail Book

J. A. Grohusko

ISBN: 978-1-880954-28-7

Classic Cocktail Guides
and Retro Bartender Books

The Twentieth-Century Guide for Mixing Fancy Drinks

A Pre-Prohibition Cocktail Book

James C. Maloney

ISBN: 978-1-880954-29-4

Classic Cocktail Guides
and Retro Bartender Books

The Ideal Bartender

Cocktails and Mixed Drinks
from the Years of the First World War

Tom Bullock
Bartender of the Pendennis Club, Louisville, Kentucky
and of the St. Louis Country Club

Introduction by George H. Walker
Grandfather to President George Herbert Walker Bush
and Great-Grandfather to President George Walker Bush

ISBN: 978-1-880954-31-7

Classic Cocktail Guides
and Retro Bartender Books

Nineteenth-Century Cocktail Creations

How to Mix Drinks: A Bar Keeper's Handbook

George Winter

ISBN: 978-1-880954-30-0

Printed in Great Britain
by Amazon.co.uk, Ltd.,
Marston Gate.